Witho...
Dubli...

D1394450

?3 CLON

Clonakilty and the Rebellion of 1798

Maynooth Studies in Local History

SERIES EDITOR Raymond Gillespie

This volume is one of six short books published in the Maynooth Studies in Local History series in 2009. Like their predecessors their aim is to explore aspects of the local experience of the Irish past. That local experience is not a simple chronicling of events that took place within a narrow set of administrative or geographically determined boundaries. Rather the local experience in the past encompasses all aspects of how local communities of people functioned from birth to death and from the pinnacle of the social order to its base. The study of the local past is as much about the recreation of mental worlds as about the reconstruction of physical ones. It tries to explore motives and meanings as well as the material context for people's beliefs. What held social groups together and what drove them apart are of equal interest and how consensus was achieved and differences managed can help to lay bare the lineaments of the local experience. The subject matter of these short books ranges widely from north Cork to the gypsum mines of Monaghan yet they have in common an exploration of different types of local societies. The world of Dublin with all its variations is revealed through an examination of one year in the life of the city (1707) and in another instance through one rather particular type of local world that was an important part of the make up of the city, the liberties. Again the reactions of the inhabitants of the city to an unflattering portrait of their world by one 18th-century traveller reveals how they discovered what they had in common in what is usually regarded as a period of division. Against this the violence associated with the murder of the Franks family in north Cork and the 1798 rebellion in Clonsilla reveal how local communities dealt with the stresses and strains of everyday life and how these could both be contained and explode into apparently random criminal activities. Despite these violent outbreaks, everyday life required the forging of alliances and understandings that allowed local societies to work. Understanding the shared assumptions that held communities together despite the tremendous pressures to which they were subjected is best done at the local level. Such communities remain the key to reconstructing how people, at many spatial and social levels, lived their lives in the past. Such research is at the forefront of Irish historical scholarship and these short books, together with the earlier titles in the series, represent some of the most innovative and exciting work being done in Irish history today. They provide models that others can use and adapt in their own studies of the local past. If these short books convey something of the enthusiasm and excitement that such studies can generate then they will have done their work well.

Maynooth Studies in Local History: Number 84

Clonsilla and the Rebellion of 1798

Ciarán Priestley

Ballymun Library Tel: 8421890

FOUR COURTS PRESS

Set in 10pt on 12pt Bembo by
Carrigboy Typesetting Services for
FOUR COURTS PRESS LTD
7 Malpas Street, Dublin 8, Ireland
e-mail: info@fourcourtspress.ie
http://www.fourcourtspress.ie
and in North America for
FOUR COURTS PRESS
c/o ISBS, 920 N.E. 58th Avenue, Suite 300, Portland, OR 97213.

© Ciarán Priestley 2009

ISBN 978-1-84682-192-9

All rights reserved. Without limiting the rights under
copyright reserved alone, no part of this publication
may be reproduced, stored in or introduced into a
retrieval system, or transmitted, in any form or by any
means (electronic, mechanical, photocopying, recording
or otherwise), without the prior written permission
of both the copyright owner and the above publisher
of this book.

Printed in England by
Athenaeum Press Ltd., Gateshead, Tyne & Wear.

George Cummins, a popish yeoman of the Clonsillagh corps, who became a traitor on the breaking-out of the rebellion, led a party of rebels (who) attacked and entered Mr Blair's extensive iron works at Lucan, carried off a considerable quantity of arms and ammunition and compelled some of his artificers to attend them to the hill of Tara.
Sir Richard Musgrave (1801)

In Memory of Seamus Ryan,
1983–2007

Contents

Acknowledgments

I would like to offer my sincere thanks to C.J. Woods for his advice, patience and enthusiasm during this research and writing process. The hospitality and professionalism of the staff of the Representative Church Body Library was of great help during the time spent investigating their unique archives. I am also grateful for the assistance of the staff at the National Library, National Archives and Blanchardstown Library. The information provided by David Parsons on his family heritage was helpful and insightful. I would also like to thank James Kelly for taking time to discuss my research and study objectives. It remains for me to thank the staff and management of St Ciarán's National School and Blakestown Community School, in whose employment I completed this work. I wish to extend my gratitude to Professor Raymond Gillespie for affording me the opportunity to complete this research as part of the MA in Local History course.

Introduction

Many of the communities which once resided in the parish of Clonsilla, Co. Dublin, have been long since forgotten, without having received significant recognition of their lives, failings and achievements in the area. While remnants and reminders of their age dot the current landscape in a variety of forms, the busy commuter suburb which inhabits the same space as the 18th-century hamlet has imposed its own identity on the land, inhabitants and place names of the area. Several local history publications have provided vital accounts of previous generations in the parishes of north-west Dublin; chief amongst them are James O'Driscoll's *Cnucha*, Jim Lacey's *Candle in the window* and Charles and Mary Mulgraine's *St Mochta's Church, Porterstown*. Each of these works summarizes the depth of knowledge available on the locality as a whole over a considerable period of time. The aim of this small book is to examine a particular community which existed in Clonsilla at a specific point in time, on the eve of the United Irish rebellion of 1798. In order to better understand the values and beliefs of these people, their actions and reactions to significant events will be contrasted with the ideology which underpinned the disturbances and insurrection which defined the late 18th century.

Fortunately, much of the primary source material which exists on this subject originates from the inhabitants of Clonsilla themselves. The manner in which they recorded the proceedings of various local associations, societies and committees means that it has been possible to allow that community convey their story with their own words. The Representative Church Body Library in Churchtown, Dublin, contains an invaluable source of local material which has been exploited during this study. The Rebellion Papers, located in the National Archives of Ireland, provide much of the sources regarding the government's outlook on events and disturbances and also provide telling insights into how their national policies were translated to the local and individual context. The National Library of Ireland contains several maps which have proved vital in pinpointing the geographical situation of the parish and surroundings. Taylor and Skinner's 18th-century road maps of Ireland also serve this purpose. The absence of significant landmarks or public buildings may make it difficult for a modern inhabitant of Dublin 15 to relate to the events outlined in this study. However, these maps are crucial in establishing the persistence of several townland names, parish borders and road directions, thus facilitating that task and portraying a more accurate picture of contemporary surroundings. In order to provide a valid account of the community which resided in Clonsilla on the eve of the United Irish rebellion of 1798, it is necessary first to examine the political and social situation of Ireland as a whole and the nature of local society in particular.

In the decade after the French Revolution in 1789, the ideology which underpinned that event swept across Europe and popular support for 'French' principles spread fear among every European government and ruling class. 'Liberté, Egalité, and Fraternité' was to become the rallying cry for a generation of ambitious young revolutionaries, eager to address the acute social problems of that time by deposing the established order, overthrowing the existing civil power and forming a republic of free citizens in which every man was to be viewed as equal in the eyes of society. Support for these principles in the Irish context manifested itself as opposition to the 'Protestant Ascendancy', a term given to the Irish political ruling class who were drawn exclusively from the Protestant section of society.

In the age of the notorious Penal Laws, which reinforced Protestant dominance over Catholics in the realms of political rights, access to professions, inheritance laws and religious freedom, the Protestant Ascendancy had jealously guarded their right to govern the country throughout the 18th-century, a claim given legitimacy following the victory of the Williamite forces at the battle of the Boyne in 1690. In the opinion of James Kelly, 'the *raison d'être* of conservative Protestant political thought in late 18th-century Ireland was to provide the "Protestant interest" with an ideological rationale to enable it to justify its dominant position in the Irish constitution'.[1] Needless to say, this was not a political body that responded favourably to any criticism of its right to govern, however frivolous it might appear to be.

The Society of United Irishmen, a club of like-minded individuals who welcomed members from every religious persuasion, came together to discuss their political and social views, not to mention their frustration at the inept landlord government in power at that time. The original club was formed in Belfast in October 1791, the beginnings of which are believed to lie in the 1791 celebrations of Bastille Day in the town.[2] Branches of the organization were soon to appear in various forms in other parts of the country. At this point, the United Irishmen consisted mainly of respectable bodies of educated, middleclass, professional men and men of small property who sought increased political influence and a share of the decision making process, to which they felt entitled. The power and influence of the Belfast club was increasingly lost to the Dublin branch, and this coincided with a growing militancy within the movement. Enigmatic young leaders such as Theobald Wolfe Tone, Henry Joy McCracken and Lord Edward FitzGerald, who themselves were of quite affluent backgrounds, attracted popular support and became national figureheads for the United Irish movement. They sported 'cropped' haircuts in the style of the French revolutionaries and their youth, ambition and sensitivity to current fashion trends ensured that United Irishmen were, to a large extent, *à la mode* for a considerable part of that decade. Also, as the leadership of the organization tended towards the more radical elements, links with the Defenders began to be forged. The Defenders were a secret, oath-based, agrarian agitation group who espoused vague political notions of reversing the contemporary trend of Protestant dominance, but more often sought to address local concerns through violent acts and intimidatory tactics.

In a strictly legal sense, Ireland at this time was an independent country. To be more precise, it was a kingdom aligned with the kingdom of Great Britain. A distinctive form of Protestant nationalism, sometimes referred to as 'colonial nationalism' and similar to that being experienced in Britain's North American colonies, had emerged in the latter decades of the 18th century. Consequently, Irish Protestants had agitated for political reforms and greater legislative freedom from the British parliament. In Henry Grattan, who entered the Irish parliament at College Green in 1775, that movement found an inspired and capable leader. Specifically, the limitations on the powers of the Irish parliament imposed by Poynings' law, and the act of 1720 declaring the right of the British parliament to legislate for Ireland, were targeted. While he believed that Ireland should be granted its rightful status as an independent nation, Grattan always insisted that Ireland should remain linked to Great Britain by a common crown and by sharing a common political tradition.[3] As such, the lord lieutenant, who resided in the Viceregal Lodge (modern day Áras an-Uachtaráin) in the Phoenix Park, represented the king and was appointed by the British government. Through his right to select and control the Irish executive, he indirectly had power over such concerns as the granting of peerages and pensions, which ensured satisfactory British control over Irish affairs.

In this optimistic climate and era of 'Grattan's parliament', many of the rarely-enforced penal laws relating to religious, social and economic well-being began to be formally and cautiously removed. Still, few would have agreed with granting the Catholic population a share in political power. Dublin began to show outward signs of its new capital city status and it was in the 1790s that the Custom House and Four Courts were built. The economic optimism of the era was epitomized by the construction of the impressive canals which ran from the Liffey in Dublin, through many of that county's neighbourhoods and provincial towns, linking eventually to the Shannon, thus dramatically opening up new trade and transport links to travellers and entrepreneurs alike.

Clonsilla (or Clonsillagh, as it was often recorded) was a parish in the barony of Castleknock in Co. Dublin, located ten kilometres north-west of the metropolis. The county of Dublin was a separate administrative unit from the city of Dublin and the barony of Castleknock was one of nine which it comprised. Lewis's *Topographical dictionary of Ireland* (1837), describes the parish as comprising of 2,943 statute acres, 'the whole of which is arable land'.[4]

According to the census of 1821, the first attempt at comprehensive national census to be completed and published, the total population of Clonsilla was 718, with an even distribution between the sexes. While it is impossible to draw definitive conclusions from a population count taken over 20 years after the events of this study, it is reasonable to assume that the same general employment patterns and livelihoods existed then, as, despite the advent of the Royal Canal and possible discovery of mineral sources along its route, no substantial evidence pertaining to a dramatic transformation of the local economy is to be found in relevant primary or secondary sources. Occupations were recorded in the 1821 census under three broad categories: 'agriculture', 'trades, manufactures or handicrafts' and 'not comprised in the preceding classes'. What we are not told is whether these statistics included women.[5] According to local records, it would also appear that women held no positions of civic responsibility within the community. Church records show that their place in a male dominated respectable society was restricted to that of daughters, wives, mothers and widows. They were, in short, defined by their relationship to men.

In the county of Dublin, those listed as employed chiefly in agriculture represented 30% of the total persons occupied. The returns for trades, manufactures or handicrafts were 32%, whereas those not comprised in the preceding classes were at 38%. Higher concentrations of skilled and manufacturing workers were traditionally located in densely populated areas, and as such Co. Dublin could be described as an area in which the transition from an urban way of life to a rural one took place. Returns for Castleknock indicated that 49% were working in agriculture, emphasizing the rural nature of the barony as a whole. A mere 13% were employed in trades, manufactures or handicrafts and the same percentage of 38% were otherwise occupied.[6i] In Clonsilla, 54% of the population was employed in agriculture and 37% was recorded as being otherwise occupied. The remaining 9% were employed in trades, manufactures or handicraft. The results for Clonsilla show a continuation of this trend towards an overwhelmingly agricultural way of life.

The total population for the county of Dublin was recorded as 150,011. The population distribution is outlined in table 1 below.

Table 1. Population in the county of Dublin, 1821

Balrothery	18,395	Donore	11,207	Rathdown	18,046
Castleknock	6,776	Nethercross	7,915	St Sepelchure's	13,179
Coolock	33,943	Newscastle	19,344	Uppercross	21,206

As can be seen in table 1, Castleknock is the least populated barony in the county of Dublin. Within Castleknock itself there are 10 subdivisions of parish and village, of which Clonsilla, with a population of 718, represented approximately 10% of the overall population of the barony. Therefore, the mean population of the parishes in the barony of Castleknock would have been similar to that found in Clonsilla.

The village of Clonsilla lies on the periphery of Dublin's borders with Meath and Kildare. Considering its geographical location, along with the breakdown of occupations in the area, a picture emerges of an overwhelmingly rural society in which over half its population made their living through agriculture. It is therefore logical to assume that Clonsilla's inhabitants interacted as much with its rural surroundings and neighbouring counties as it did with its city and urban links.

1. Civic initiative and parish politics in Clonsilla, 1792–7

When Weston St John Joyce was compiling and publishing a series of guided walks around the neighbourhoods of Co. Dublin in the 1890s, he remarked of Clonsilla that

> there is nothing worthy of the name of a village or hamlet here; the place consists of a few scattered cottages and an extremely pretty church … the railway station is in fact the most important feature, and probably it alone has preserved the place from utter oblivion.[1]

Having arrived in the village from Dunboyne, he wasted little time in guiding the Victorian rambler out of Clonsilla, over Callaghan's humpback bridge and along the road to the Luttrellstown demesne and back to Lucan. St John Joyce's initial impression of Clonsilla was, in all likelihood, not dissimilar to current attitudes to the area. Dismissive, unimpressed and failing to notice any real character, the visitor passes swiftly through on to other, more worthwhile, destinations. Undoubtedly, Clonsilla's lack of public buildings, civic projects or long standing memorials give the impression that it is an area devoid of history or notable occasion in the past. What a short journey through the area cannot appreciate, however, is the richness of the communities that reside within. Ever evolving, subject to sharp rises and dramatic falls, the demographics of Clonsilla throughout the past three centuries are reflective of the social structures and local influences experienced across Ireland as a whole.

The main subject of this study is of the community which existed in Clonsilla 100 years prior to St John Joyce's visit. On the eve of the 1798 Rebellion, this community lived in an era in which social unrest and mutual distrust and hatred between the factions of society was so endemic that an uprising in search of the universal rights of man, and a consequent suppression carried out in order to protect power, property and family, was to descend into a frenzy of sectarian violence, murder and barbarity. Despite the island's turbulent and eventful history, few events were to have as important an effect on subsequent generations and popular opinion as those which surrounded the United Irish rebellion of 1798.

A map of the proposed route of the Royal Canal was drafted in 1791 and it appears to have been drawn for the purpose of assessing who was to be in receipt of compensation owing to the path of the canal crossing their lands. It

1 St Mary's Church, Clonsilla

outlined the intended passage through the village of Clonsilla.[2] Seemingly, John Binns, who sat on the board of directors of the Grand Canal Company, was suitably angered by a perceived attack on his character and position by his fellow board members, who reportedly called him 'a cobbler', that he hastily departed his seat by telling them 'You may think me a very insignificant person, but I will show you the contrary. I will sell out forthwith, start a rival canal, and carry all the traffic.' Binns supposedly convinced a number of west Dublin gentlemen to back his canal venture from Dublin to Mullingar, and petitions were presented to the house of commons in 1789 seeking aid to build the newly proposed canal and on 24 October of that year the Royal Canal Company was enrolled. The canal itself was said to have cost five times its original estimate and one of the most controversial stretches was known as the 'deep sinking' between Blanchardstown and Clonsilla. It cost approximately £40,000 to blast through the hard block of calcareous stone which was embedded in that area.[3] That stone is clearly visible along the canal bank to this day.

Chief among the canal's backers was Henry Lawes Luttrell, the 2nd earl of Carhampton, current head of the Luttrell family, owner of much of the lands of Clonsilla and occupier of Luttrellstown Castle and demesne. Sir Geoffrey Luttrell was the first member of the Luttrell family to come to Ireland with King John in 1210 and the family's connection to the area would seem to date from then.[4] To say that the Luttrell family had gained a dubious reputation during this time would be an understatement. A passage from the *Letters of Junius* (1769–71) seems to best typify popular opinion towards the family at that time. It reads:

> there is a certain family in this county on which nature seems to have entailed a hereditary base of disposition. As far as their history has been known, the son has regularly improved upon the vices of his father, and has taken care to transmit them pure and undiminished into the bosom of his successor.[5]

Locally, the Luttrells' reputation was such that it was believed that Simon Luttrell, father of Henry Lawes Luttrell, had sold his soul to the devil in return for the overnight construction of a mill, on the banks of the Liffey along the road to Lucan from his demesne. To this day that mill is known locally as 'the devil's mill'. The transaction is said to have been agreed, although never honoured, in the notorious Hellfire Club in the Wicklow mountains. Locals attributed Luttrell's rumoured inability to cast a shadow to his dealings with such unsavoury business partners. In 1717, Carhampton's grandfather Henry, a traitor to the Jacobite cause, was assassinated by persons unknown in Dublin en route to his house in Stafford Street.[6] The 2nd earl of Carhampton is said to have enjoyed a rather tempestuous relationship with his own father, who once challenged him to a duel with the invitation 'if you can forget that I am your father'. It is said that the son responded 'My Lord, I wish I could at any time forget that you are my father'.[7] Many of the Catholic inhabitants of Clonsilla are said to have been tenants of the earl of Carhampton,[8] and while outward compliance and an apparent subjugation to so powerful a landlord is probable, it is equally likely that this masked a deep-seated loathing of their landlord. That he had, in his lifetime, narrowly escaped conviction for the abduction and rape of a child can have done little to tackle his perceived predisposition to hereditary debauchery.[9]

On 22 March 1792, the 'Association of the Inhabitants of the United Parishes of Castleknock, Leixlip, Chapelizod and Dunboyne' was formed at the Royal Exchange in Dublin. The concerned gentlemen of these separate parishes felt compelled to 'adopt extraordinary measures for the protection of (their) persons and properties' following 'the frequent outrages in many parts of this united district'. On that day, the gentlemen present passed several resolutions in response to these activities, chief among them to 'pay the sum of £50 over and above all rewards offered by government' and '£20 to any persons who shall detect and apprehend any in the act of carrying away or thieving any part of plundered property'.[10] To put that amount in context, the annual salary of James Lyons, the clerk of Clonsilla church, was £10 in 1792.[11]

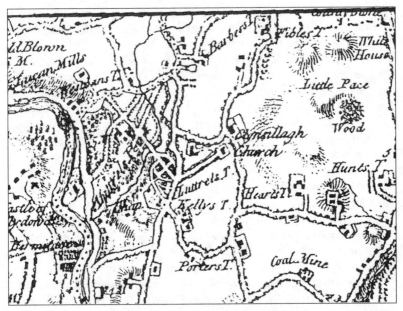

2 The townlands surrounding Clonsilla church
(John Rocque's map of county Dublin).

The Association acted as a neighbourhood watch, of sorts, in the areas outlined in its title. It resolved to 'collectively and individually give immediate assistance when called upon by any inhabitant of the aforesaid parishes to apprehend or pursue any offender or gang of suspicious persons who may be pointed out to us in any quarter of this united district'.

In 'Defenderism', the gentlemen of these previously unrelated districts faced a common enemy against which it was necessary to unite. The first page of the Association minute book states their determination to pursue 'every person who shall kill, cut open or skin any bull, ox, cow ... with an intent to steal the whole, or any part of the fat, flesh, skin or carcase' (all traditional night time Defender activities) to the full rigours of the law. At this time, to be convicted of such crimes carried a sentence of death, 'without the benefit of clergy'.[12] On that first meeting of the Association, 69 signatories in total contributed a monetary subscription determined by their respective status and wealth. The earl of Carhampton's subscription amounted to £22 15s. 0d. whereas the secretary of state, J.H. Hutchinson, contributed £10. Prominent local gentlemen such as Alexander Kirkpatrick, Francis McFarland, Robert Wynne and Walter Troy each paid £5 13s. 9d. Despite paying the same subscription as the vast majority of Association members, and notwithstanding the large geographical area covered, the exertions and consistency of the aforementioned gentlemen ensured that the Association, to a large extent, became Clonsilla

dominated during the 1790s. A combination of different factors culminated in
a situation whereby, post-rebellion, meetings were held exclusively in Clonsilla
and dealt almost exclusively with parish disturbances.

Alexander Kirkpatrick had bought Robert Bolton's estate at Coolmine for
£14,500 in 1782. He was a director of the Royal Canal Company and his
family were said to be wealthy wool merchants who had originated in
Scotland.[13] The parish register recorded that his wife, Mary, gave birth to a
child in 1792. Elizabeth Kirkpatrick was the eldest of three daughters, Margaret
and Anne being born in 1793 and 1794 respectively.[14] He seems also to have
had a son, Alexander, who was born at an earlier date. Kirkpatrick was to play
a very active role in the Association and in the community as a whole. As new
organizations and initiatives were begun locally, he was chief among the earliest
signatories and also acquired several administrative roles. Indeed, at an
Association meeting on 1 November 1792 which he presided over, he was
appointed treasurer in place of Robert Mahon Wade and entrusted to resolve
the recurring problems relating to the collection of members' subscriptions.
He was granted permission to employ someone for this purpose and at a meeting
on 7 December 1792, it was decided to pay this individual the commission of
1s. of every £1 collected.[15] His vested interest was his significant land holding
and tenant base; hence his role in such organizations and his public spirit is
unsurprising when all things are considered. One other such gentleman and
prominent member of the Association was Francis McFarland. A 1794 survey
of the lands of Lord Carhampton let to Henry Blackwood in Castaheaney,
around two kilometres to the east of Clonsilla, shows the significant land
holding McFarland held in that area. According to a map surveying the lands
of Capt. George Vesey in Westmanstown on 20 July 1796, McFarland also held
a considerable portion of land on the road between Clonsilla and Lucan, about
one kilometre from Clonsilla church on Carhampton's Lutrellstown demesne.[16]
He was a regular and productive attendee of meetings and often directed
proceedings from the chair. As a widely respected elderly gentleman with a
large family in the localty, McFarland, in his sixties by 1792, seemed the ideal
candidate for such a sensitive and impartial role.

In order to illustrate how the Association intended to function, it is
necessary to investigate the first major 'outrage' to occur in the newly united
districts and how this first challenge was dealt with by the members. At a
meeting in Kearns Hotel in Lucan on 7 June 1792, George Vesey, in the chair,
reported that:

> a burglary, rape and robbery attended with some circumstances of great
> barbarity has been committed by a gang of ruffians in the parish of
> Castleknock since the establishment of this association, and whereas the
> only person taken up on suspicion of being concerned with the said

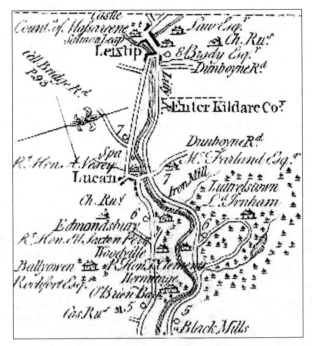

3 Taylor and Skinner's map of Clonsilla, showing the
lands of Francis McFarland

outrage has been freed and acquitted – [it is] resolved that every effort
of this association be exerted until the persons guilty of the said offences
be brought to justice.[17]

The meeting also approved sums of two guineas to be paid to a Clonsilla
gentleman, Peter Jackson, for attempting to prosecute Patrick Daly for the
crime and the same also was paid to the Revd David Bricketh, Protestant
curate of Clonsilla, for the purpose of 'obtaining private information' relating
to the gang. The significance of the meeting can be measured by the fact that
the earl of Carhampton was in attendance, and as was always the case when
the earl was present, the signature of Robert Wynne appeared on the register.
A letter sent to Major William Brady by Bricketh on behalf of the Association
on 8 June reads:

> I feel very sensible satisfaction in conveying to you the unanimous vote
> of thanks for your spirited and very active exertions in endeavouring to
> apprehend the gang of desperate ruffians who committed the late
> atrocities of robbery and rape on the widow Tiernan – when offended
> laws of the country have such magistrates determined to support their

dignity and enforce the strict sense of justice, the poor may live secure
of meeting redress for their wrongs, and the daring villain will shrink
from the committal of those crimes that must bring down inevitable
punishment on his own hand.[18]

The determined magistrates enamoured response, sent from Leixlip the
following day, thanked the gentlemen of the Association 'for the great honour
they have done me in approving so highly of my endeavours in the execution
of my duty to bring the villains to justice'. While she undoubtedly would have
felt a certain sense of satisfaction in knowing that her affliction had allowed
the officers of justice and the propertied gentlemen of the Association to
correspond in such a noble and affectionate manner, as of yet, there was no
report on the condition of the widow Tiernan.

On 7 December 1792, the Association agreed that Bricketh be paid 'such
sums as he has advanced to the persons who apprehended and lodged in
Kilmainham Gaol the body of Daniel Leals, charged with housebreaking and
rape'. An undated entry from 1793 details a reward of £30 to be paid to John
and Thomas Butler, Michael Connolly and James and John Tiernan for
apprehending Daniel Leals, and a further £20 be paid to E. Tiernan 'for
prosecuting to conviction Daniel Leals'. Although there is no evidence of any
family connection between the aforementioned Tiernans and the unfortunate
widow of the same name, it is tempting to speculate whether the Association,
through payment from Bricketh and by appealing to relatives directly affected
by the crime, encouraged a robust means of 'community justice' in order to
ensure that the authorities could deal satisfactorily with the case in the eyes of
the law. That the perpetrators were, up until this point, referred to as a 'gang'
seemed irrelevant once justice was seen to be served and the case was never
again referred to in the Association minute book.[19]

A sense of how the ascendancy mind translated to local issues also emerged
from this case – a distinct detachment from the actual people affected by the
crime is endemic in every entry related to it. Although not formally recorded,
it is possible that the widow was in receipt of private assistance from the
landlord of whom she was a tenant. Despite a clear resolve to punish those, or
someone found to be, responsible for the crime perpetrated on the widow
Tiernan, it seems, at times, to have been pursued more from a sense of duty
and a desire to uphold public order rather than from a personal concern for
the victim.

Prior to the establishment of the Association, January 1792 had seen the
first issue of the *Northern Star*, an Ulster newspaper edited by Samuel Neilson.
It quickly became the popular voice of the United Irishmen. In February, a
petition from the Catholic pressure group, the Catholic Committee, for
parliamentary franchise and other concessions for its members, was rejected

by the Irish parliament by 208 votes to 25. In April of the same year, the Catholic Relief Act allowed Catholics to practise as lawyers. The political mood and public opinion of the time can be measured by the series of daily notices which appeared in the *Freeman's Journal* throughout the later months of 1792, in response to Edward Byrne's proposals for Catholics to elect representative bodies. One such response, from the freeholders of Kerry, reads

> although we have seen with satisfaction the progression of public opinion in favour of our Catholic brethren we cannot but consider any efforts made upon the Catholics of this kingdom to assemble themselves collectively or representatively as calculated to continue and preserve separate views and interests between Catholics and Protestants[20]

Numerous notices of similar sentiment from freeholders, high sheriffs and grand juries of towns and counties across the country were printed in every edition from this period. By January 1793, the proprietors of the *Northern Star* had been charged with sedition.

Internationally, the execution of Louis XVI of France took place on 21 January, followed by France's declaration of war on Britain and Holland on 1 February. An Association meeting on 5 March was adjourned and business not entered into, owing to an insufficient number of members having attended. Despite the relative international turmoil of the time, a general sense of malaise appears to have set in regarding local issues as the initial enthusiasm for the Association seems to have waned. During the following meeting, it was decided to issue an ultimatum to expel all members who had not paid their subscription by 17 April.

The vestry minute books for Clonsilla church record on 21 May that church wardens Walter Troy and Thomas Bryan were to 'pay to Revd Bricketh the sum of £3 1s. 0d., the amount of salary due to the late James Lyons ... sum is to be given to said Lyons child, at present a minor'. Lyons had been employed by the parish with his wife Sarah, both at the annual salary of £10, and had recently completed the task of whitewashing the church and repairing the ceiling. For this purpose he had been advanced £2 16s. 10d. in expenses on 28 May 1792.[21]

A classic case of Defender activity visited the parish towards the end of 1793 and two separate incidents were addressed at an Association meeting, chaired for the first time by Robert Wynne on 22 November. After further discussion with regards to the collection of subscriptions, it was reported that on the night of 23 October, two sheep, the property of Robert Wynne, were killed on the lands of Clonsillagh. Also, on the night of the 20th, three sheep were killed on the lands of Francis McFarland. During the same meeting, it was resolved to pay the sum of £50 to any person 'who shall within six months from the date hereof discover or prosecute to conviction, persons concerned in the above mentioned inhumane practices'.[22] Through the local associations, Wynne was to prove himself a very capable administrator. The initiative he displayed in calling and chairing the Association meeting following the attack on his property demonstrated his ability to use the Association productively for his own ends, and this was a constant theme of his public life throughout this period.

Robert was the fourth son of the powerful Wynne family of Hazelwood, Co. Sligo. The family was of Welsh heritage, but had settled in Ireland during the 17th century and acquired their Sligo estate in 1722. For 300 years, the head of the family, with one exception, was the eldest son who bore the forename of Owen.[23] As the fourth son, Robert would have held no realistic expectation of inheriting the family estate. It is likely that he moved to Dublin with the intention of establishing himself in the capital by virtue of his work ethic, ambition and family connections. Born in 1760, he married Elizabeth Singleton of Drogheda around 30 years later. According to parish registers, Elizabeth had given birth to the couple's third surviving child in 1793. Emily Wynne was preceded by Robert in 1792 and Harriet in 1791. Their family grew consistently during the first decade of the Wynne's marriage, Lucy being born in 1794, John in 1796 and Francis in 1800.[24] The couple also suffered the loss of two children at this time, Sydenham died in infancy in 1794 and James died in 1800.[25]

Bricketh, curate of Clonsilla, made an entry on Easter Monday 1794 into the vestry minute books which detailed that Robert Wynne and Peter Jackson were to be appointed church wardens 'in the room of Mr W. Troy and Tho[ma]s Bryan, late wardens who not settling their account for the last two years of their office'.[26] A member of the Association for the Protection of Private Property, Peter Jackson had failed to secure the conviction of Patrick Daly for the robbery and rape of the widow Tiernan two years previously. The Mr Troy in question was in fact Walter Troy, also a member of the Association and brother to the then Catholic archbishop of Dublin, John Thomas Troy. The family originated in Annfield, in a house which stood facing the present Porterstown Catholic church only a few kilometres from Clonsilla. Evidently, they were a prosperous family as they also held a house at Smithfield in Dublin, which at that time also counted the earl of Bective as one of its inhabitants. John Troy was the eldest of seven children and at 16 he was sent to study in Rome where he distinguished himself over a period of 21 years.[27] While John had established himself as a scholar of some note overseas at a time when Irish Catholics still had to travel abroad for higher education, Walter had remained as a farmer in the area. While he was himself a Catholic, he may have taken on the role of church warden of the local established church as a means of advancing his position in the local community. Due to the close legal relationship between state and established church, the position of warden was also effectively that of government agent. The role involved managing the parish account books and outgoings, thus involving important monetary trusts and responsibilities. A reputable Catholic may have taken on the role to publicly display and demonstrate his loyalty and respectability.

The first vestry meeting after the appointment of Wynne and Jackson took place on 1 May 1794. It was immediately adjourned owing to the 'late church wardens not appearing with their respective accounts'. The next meeting, attended by Carhampton on 29 May, sought to 'take into consideration some effectual means of repairing and enlarging this Church which is at present much out of repair and found to be too small at present to contain the usual congregation'.[28] This entry would explain the pressing need for clarity in terms of parish finances. Elements of a village scandal were in evidence as both former wardens were again summoned to return their accounts on 9 June, but they failed to appear. The attendance of the earl at the 29 May meeting indicates the significance of this issue from a local perspective and his involvement should have exerted suitable pressure upon the former wardens to settle their accounts at the earliest possible convenience. It is conceivable that a considerable amount of local debate would have surrounded the issue, compounded by the former wardens repeated failure to clarify the parish finances. When the accounts were eventually settled on 17 June, it is interesting to note that the signatures of the former wardens appear last on the registry, highlighting their humble and compromised position during that night's proceedings. On that same evening, Thomas Kernan and George Harvey were appointed constable and parish clerk respectively. In advance of the repair and enlargement of the church, it is logical to assume that competent and trustworthy candidates would have been sought by the vestry to manage parish finances. Such a commitment, if successfully undertaken, would undoubtedly advance one's position in the local community while suitably impressing a figure of such national standing as the earl of Carhampton.

National news in 1794 was dominated by the suppression of the United Irishmen. The political mood had been affected by the ongoing war with France and the fear that the republican aspirations of the United Irishmen made them likely accomplices to a French invasion. These concerns were not unfounded as in April, the Revd William Jackson, agent of the French revolutionary government, was arrested in Dublin on a charge of high treason. He was to commit suicide while still in custody over a year later. In May, the Dublin United Irish premises at Tailor's Hill were raided, resulting in some of the Dublin society's membership taking flight. The popular base of the Belfast society made suppression less effective there. Towards the end of the year, the Northern United Irish Society composed an oath, calling for 'an equal, full and adequate representation of all the people of Ireland' to be taken by its members. This effectively meant that the United Irishmen were now a mass-based secret society, ensuring that its membership base was likely to become increasingly intertwined with that of the Defenders. It is important to remember, however, that in March 1794 the statutes of Dublin University had been amended to allow Catholics to take degrees. Despite the heightened political and religious tensions of the period, there were still people of influence who sought to maintain public order by addressing the existing social imbalances and legitimate concerns of the disenfranchised. In this climate, Walter Troy was either a victim of his eldest brother's illustrious position or his own questionable bookkeeping.

An 'extraordinary meeting of the landholders and inhabitants of the parish of Clonsilla' took place on 29 April 1795 in St Mary's church, Clonsilla. The purpose of the meeting was to 'take into consideration the most effectual means of conforming to the late militia act of parliament', an act which impressed upon a locality to provide a portion of the adequate number of able bodied men deemed necessary to ensure the defence of the country. As a community, the response of the people of Clonsilla to this requirement was striking. At that meeting it was decided to levy the sizeable sum of £35, 'at the agreeable rate of five pence per acre' of each inhabitant's landholding. This money was to be paid 'into the hands of the treasurer of the county of Dublin to provide substitutes for the six men drawn by ballot as the quota of men to be furnished by this parish'.[29] It was sought to bring this issue to a positive outcome collectively, and by a means which ensured that each individual contributed an equal proportion of their personal wealth. However, while the noble aspirations of the vestry members were formally recorded, it is impossible to know whether this view was shared by all in the locality. This new levy may have been viewed by others in the area as merely another government tax, collected locally by members of the established church.

The following month, on 26 May, Robert Wynne and Peter Jackson were reappointed church wardens for another year. On that day, Wynne promptly settled his account with a favourable balance of £8. 2s. 4d. 'over and above all charges'.[30] Bricketh, undoubtedly relieved after the previous year's debacle, empowered 'said Robert Wynne to expend the said balance in enclosing the church yard in such manner as he may take necessary advantage'.[31] Confidence suitably instilled, Wynne was granted permission to undertake important parish business on the basis of his own respected judgment. Three days later, with the earl of Carhampton in the chair, he was appointed secretary of the Association for the Protection of Private Property for one year.[32]

Carhampton was praised in the *Freeman's Journal* of 26 May 1795 on the same day Wynne settled his parish account in credit. Its owner, Francis Higgins, was already supplying Dublin castle with gossip. He was singled out for his vigorous (and illegal) campaign against the Defenders in Connacht which resulted in the forced enlistment of hundreds in the Royal Navy. Local magistrates had been encouraged to condemn many with questionable levels of culpability to the fleet.[33] The *Freeman's Journal* had been a beacon of free speech and informed political debate before its acquisition by the notorious 'sham squire', as a judge in a fraud case once labelled Higgins after he impersonated a wealthy Catholic land owner in order to marry Maryanne Archer, the heiress daughter of a rich Catholic merchant.[34] The newspaper would go on to resume its previous position after the departure of Higgins, but for the duration of his ownership it remained little more than an organ of Castle opinion and outlook. Its rabid loathing and criticisms of 'French' principles at times boarded on the farcical, a shortage of French brandy in the country in 1792 being attributed to the fact that 'the French consume all that kind of spirit they manufacture among themselves, as their atrocities are like the ravages of intoxication'.[35] The issue of the newspaper for 17 October reported that 'Lord Carhampton, we are happy to announce is perfectly recovered from his late alarming indisposition', although details were not entered into. The same edition detailed the formation of 'the Association for the Protection of Property and the Constitution in the District of the Metropolis', to which Carhampton was a primary signatory. The 'inhabitants of the city of Dublin' pledged that they would 'at all times be ready to assist the civil power for the suppression of tumult and disorder'. They took this measure due to 'the metropolis and its neighbourhood having lately become a receptacle [for] disturbers of the peace, titling themselves Defenders'.[36]

Previous to this, the Battle of the Diamond took place near Loughgall in Co. Armagh on 21 September 1795. It was fought between the Defenders and their Protestant counterparts, the Peep o' Day Boys, and directly led to the foundation of the Orange Order. In the later months of 1795, the links between the United Irishmen and the Defenders continued to develop. Eventually, these links would progress to a point where a member of one organization was assumed to be affiliated with the other. In the opinion of Kevin Whelan, this merger created 'the great establishment nightmare of the eighteenth century – the Jacobising of the secret societies'.[37] As sectarian tensions continued to mount, however, legitimate grievances of loyal Catholics continued to be appeased, and in October 1795 the Royal College of St Patrick, a Catholic seminary, was established in Maynooth, Co. Kildare. Theobald Wolfe Tone arrived in France from the United States of America in February 1796, and was to use his considerable charisma to move in high and influential circles in order to drum up French support for an Irish expedition. The Insurrection Act, passed in March 1796, punished those found to be administering illegal oaths with the death penalty and allowed the government to impose curfews and arms searches on districts which they proclaimed to be disturbed. This draconian legislation reflected the fact that disorder was spreading throughout

1796 and a domestic military, already stretched by foreign wars and desertion, was ill equipped to deal with a national uprising and French invasion, should that occur.

On 11 February 1796, a party of up to 50 Defenders attacked the house, near the mills adjacent to the Luttrellstown demesne, of a 'poor man' named Patrick McCormick. They murdered both him and his fifteen-year-old brother, whose brains they reportedly 'beat out with the butt end of their rifle'.[38] Murders of this nature had occurred frequently around this time. Only nine days previously, the *Freeman's Journal* reported a similar incident at a small public house on the Trim road during which a husband and wife were murdered for having supplied information on local Defenders. One of the attackers was said to have 'fired a loaded bluderbuss at the unfortunate man, and being near him, shot the head off his body'. The incident near Luttrellstown, however, seems to have attracted particular attention and was widely debated in the national press and houses of parliament. It was cited by both as being symptomatic of the deterioration of law and order, the barbarity of their enemy and the gravity of the security concerns that the country now faced. McCormick had been due to give evidence for the crown at the trial of some Defenders in Dublin. A report on the trial of 'The King versus Read and White' which was published in the *Freeman's Journal* on 16 February 1796 revealed that Mr Kells, as council for the crown, had moved to postpone the trial for a second time. Previous to this, McCormick was a material witness for the crown and had been sworn to provide evidence before the grand jury. It appears that some objections were then raised as to the credibility of McCormick's intended testimony and 'because it appeared that the crown was unprepared', the trial was postponed and a date was fixed for 15 February. Unfortunately for McCormick, it was now public knowledge that he was to assist the prosecution of the defendants. A military guard had been posted on the Luttrellstown estate for the protection of local inhabitants, and it was within a few hundred yards of their post that the murder was committed. The proximity of the military explains the size of the party which arrived at McCormick's residence. Evidently, local Defenders were sufficiently confident of their ability to engage the crown forces in order to carry out their task.

The attack on McCormick indicated a ruthless efficiency on the part of Defenders to act upon such information as they received and the relative inadequacy of conventional security measures to prevent such incidents from occurring. While the crown prosecution could have been accused of woefully inadequate attention to duty, the fact still remained that Defenders were employing the due process of law, an instrument designed for their prosecution, to their own advantage. The response of government to the issue was to accelerate the debate and process that was to result in the passing of appropriate legislation. The day after the murder, Lord Dillon, speaking in the House of

Lords, cited the incident as evidence that 'if strong measures were not adopted before the rising of parliament … to wait until the next session, would be too late'.[39] In the same address, Dillon praised Carhampton's campaign in Connacht and stated his belief that the adoption of military law in disturbed districts, as it was previously understood, would be ineffective. The executive power, he felt, 'should be invested with some new authority for immediately suppressing that spirit of anarchy and rebellion that degraded the nation' and that 'such districts in which those offences prevailed should be declared out of his majesty's peace'. The day's proceedings at the House of Lords were dominated by similar statements of intent and praise from nobility across the country. Their sentiments were best summarized by the Lord Chancellor's declaration that

> the ordinary purposes of the law are incompetent to check the licentiousness of the times. If this session should pass over without the enaction of laws strong enough to meet the smothered rebellion in the country, there will be a revival of the miseries of 1641. The traitors proceed systematically to deter witnesses and make conviction impossible; how then, unless magistrates are empowered to repress treason in a summary way, can it be put to an end?[40]

On 17 May 1796, Alexander Kirkpatrick was appointed as Robert Wynne's fellow warden of Clonsilla church. During that same meeting it was recorded that the church repairs and enlargement were 'nearing completion'. A little over a month later, on 28 July, it was reported that the 'enlarging and repairing of this church being now finished and completed by the Right Honourable Earl of Carhampton at considerable expense'. The deepest gratitude of the wardens and of the parish was expressed during this meeting and a gesture of goodwill for the earl was decided upon. It was proposed that 'wardens, inhabitants and parishioners … who occupy the new seats should pay certain sums of money for their respective seats to remember him [Carhampton] in some part for his expenditure'.[41] The actual sum advanced by the earl was not alluded to, but it can be presumed to have been a significant amount as the sum total of the 'compensation' scheme proposed by the parishioners only aimed to reimburse Carhampton 'in some part'. Given his dynamic approach to such matters, it is likely that the hand of Robert Wynne was not far from this proposal. An acute awareness of how to manipulate situations to his own ends was again in evidence when the vestry raised prices for burials on its grounds. The parish felt justified in doing this as Wynne had successfully enclosed the church and surrounding graveyard behind a wall, as he was given free hand to do after he settled his account early and in credit during the previous year. A cost of 3s. 3d. was now to be incurred by parishioners who wished to be buried on the grounds whereas non-parishioners had to pay double that amount. Suitable attention is paid to ensure that Clonsilla graveyard's product improves in line with these new charges, as in addition to the new wall the sexton was 'obliged to make each grave five feet deep'. To cope with the expected increase in demand, William Dobbs was appointed grave digger, with an annual salary of three guineas, plus 'such burial fees he shall receive'.[42] The expected increase in parish revenue must have reflected favourably upon Wynne's handling of parish accounts.

In Dunboyne, a Co. Meath village about six kilometres from Clonsilla, the bodies of William Connolly and Thomas Carney were discovered on the lands of Rooske, adjoining the village between the hours of three and four in the afternoon on 7 August 1796. The coroner of the county of Meath recorded that they were killed by having their throats cut across. A recurring notice in the *Freeman's Journal*, signed by Carhampton amongst others, pledged a reward of £100 for the perpetrators of the crime.[43] An oral account, recorded and reproduced in a locally published historical journal, may shed some light on the incident in question. It reads:

> a dance was being held at the junction opposite where Dunboyne National School is now. It was being used to swear in members of the United Irishmen. This was observed by someone who immediately set out to report the occurrence to the authorities. He was seen leaving and a young man followed him up the Rooske road. The young man caught up with the would-be informer and dispatched him by cutting his throat. The young man returned to the dance with blood on his clothes. A quick-thinking young lady feigned a fight and struck the young man on the face, which bled and covered the traces of the dead man's blood.[44]

Michael Kenny's article suggests that the two areas, known locally as the 'Murdering Field' and 'Deadman's Corner', along the Rooske road may be attributed to this incident. While this oral account mentions a single assassin and victim, it is conceivable that details of the crime had been altered as it passed from generation to generation. If they were indeed separate, yet almost identical incidents, it is equally likely that similar motivations and methods were employed in the execution of both crimes.

Also in August 1796, the United Irishman Arthur O'Connor met the French general Lazare Hoche to discuss possible Irish support for an intended French invasion of Ireland. In October 1796, parliament passed the Habeas Corpus Suspension Act in response to the general spread of disorder throughout the country. This meant that any person suspected of treasonable offences could be detained by a warrant signed by the lord lieutenant. Parliament had also approved proposals for the establishment of locally-raised yeomanry corps throughout the country. Similar in ways to an army reserve force, it was expected that these bodies of loyal citizens would assist the military in case of invasion and also carry out police duties within their localities.[45]

There had been some reservations in government circles about repeating the practice of raising locally-based defence forces following the experience of the Volunteers 20 years previously. During the American war of independence, when France and Spain entered on the colonists' side, the British military were stretched to a point that an invasion of Ireland was a real possibility. In response to this, public-spirited landlords and loyal citizens formed volunteer corps across the country. Ultimately, volunteering became a fashionable pastime and reviews and parades of impressively clad part-time soldiers were a regular occurrence. As time progressed, the volunteer corps easily became political debating societies and it soon became clear that a drastic shift in power had taken place. Armed force – the ultimate arbitrator – was no longer controlled by the government but by the politically-minded public.[46] When Henry Grattan began to agitate for greater legislative freedom for Ireland around this time, his ideas spread rapidly amongst the volunteer corps. Eventually, the British authorities were obliged to concede ground to the calls for political reform and while the vast majority of Volunteers were far too respectable ever to use force against the government, it had set a dangerous and worrying precedent in terms of popular politics and the undermining of existing civil authority through intimidatory tactics.

Evidently, the establishment of the yeomanry corps sparked a similarly fervent response from loyal citizens across the country in 1796. The emphasis on the pageantry and fashion opportunities afforded by the occasion were encapsulated by an advertisement which frequently appeared in the *Freeman's Journal* around this time. Michael Murphy of 55 Fishamble Street in Dublin city enthusiastically boasted that he had the 'honour of supplying the gentlemen of the army these thirty years past, and was the first to establish a button factory in this kingdom'. His credentials firmly established, he also 'begs leave to acquaint the noblemen and gentlemen in the corps now forming, that any orders he may be favoured with shall be executed in the best manner, and on the shortest notice'.[47] The advertisement was also printed in the issue of 20 October which announced that Robert Wynne had been commissioned as captain of the Clonsilla Cavalry, with Alexander Kirkpatrick as his lieutenant.[48]

The desperation of the army's situation in October 1796 can be surmised from a declaration by the lord lieutenant which stated that 'several deserters from different regiments in this kingdom who might be induced to return to their duty … shall receive his majesty's pardon for such offences of desertion'.[49] It would appear that the commanders of the Clonsilla Cavalry experienced some local opposition to their intentions to establish an armed force in the area, as a letter sent by Francis Higgins to Dublin Castle on 29 December would indicate. It reads:

Leabharlanna Poibli Chathair Bhaile Átha Cliath
Dublin City Public Libraries

the Clonsilla Horse, many of whom are tenants to the earl of
Carhampton never have assembled because Mr Troy (brother to the
titular archbishop of Dublin) thought proper to decry the measure of
arming (after he was enrolled) and by much address the troop for the
first time meet under Mr Wynne, their officer, on tomorrow.[50]

Whether Walter Troy's motives for opposing Wynne and Kirkpatrick's
intentions to arm the inhabitants of Clonsilla were concerns he may have held
over the suitability of the rank and file of the cavalry to bear arms responsibly,
or indeed, loyally, his position must have been compromised by the fact that
Wynne had so publicly called Troy's character into question by his own
competent and dependable managing of the vestry accounts. His resolve to
oppose the commanders must surely have been broken as the news filtered
through that seven days previously, only bad weather had prevented a French
invasion fleet, with Tone on board, to effect a landing while within touching
distance of Bantry Bay, Co. Cork.

In May 1797, Clonsilla Cavalry commanders Robert Wynne and Alexander
Kirkpatrick were again returned as church wardens for the following year.[51]
On 25 May, there was an assassination attempt made on Lord Carhampton
involving two workers on the Luttrellstown demesne, James Dunn, a farmer
and blacksmith, and a labourer named Patrick Carthy. Sir Richard Musgrave
described the former as having 'constantly experienced the most striking
instances of kindness from him [Carhampton]'.[52] In his account of the plot to
assassinate the earl, Musgrave described how Dunn had attended a meeting in
the house of Maurice Dunn, a relation in Dublin, and 'offered to a committee
of sixteen United Irishmen to "do out" his friend and benefactor. This [to "do
out"] was a common cant expression United Irishmen used for murdering a
person'. From this meeting, a committee of seven were appointed to procure
weapons for the clandestine operation, which, according to Musgrave, was to
be carried out as follows:

> Three of them on horseback, having loose coats and blunderbusses under
> them, and six mounted as yeomanry cavalry with pistols, were to fire
> into his lordships carriage, as it passed through a narrow road near
> Luttrellstown, and at the same time to murder his servants and any
> persons who might be with him.

The plot was betrayed by a man named Ferris, who was the head of the United
Irish committee of sixteen, and whom Musgrave described as 'the only
Protestant member of it'. He was so 'struck with horror at the atrocity of the
plot [when he] discovered it' that he was compelled to inform on the would-
be assassins and their conspiracy. Carhampton is said to have visited Dunn in

4 Henry Lawes Luttrell, the second Earl of
Carhampton © National Gallery of Ireland.

his cell prior to his execution to express his dismay at his former friend's
devious intentions. He reportedly stated, 'considering the kindness I showed
you, I did not imagine that you would be concerned with an attempt on my
life', to which Dunn responded that he felt the assassination was 'a good act'.
Dunn also explained to the earl that while he hadn't proposed the murder, 'he
was sworn to execute it and if he were out again, he would perpetrate it if he
could'.[53] Carthy was also sent to the gallows for his part in the plot.

It is unwise to dismiss Carhampton's sense of personal betrayal at Dunn's
intentions as having been entirely due to his own naivety and poor judgment.
The acute social separation of landlord and tenant was potentially mirrored by
a gulf of understanding in that relationship. Acts of charity may have bred
resentment on the part of the benefactor; acts of kindness were possibly
interpreted as a sign of weakness. Such a phenomenon might be understood
when the inequality of society at that time is considered, a political structure
in which minority rule was a reality. The local gentry aspired to entrust
responsibility and arms into the hands of tenants in the area, hoping that their
good faith would be rewarded with loyalty and obedience. The details of the
assassination plot on the earl indicated that these intentions may have been lost
in social translation.

This high-profile attempt aside, Carhampton had been conspicuous by his
frequent absences from local affairs at this time. This was due, in no small part,
to the fact that during much of 1796 and 1797, he was commander-in-chief

of the armed forces of the crown in Ireland. Befitting to his reputation, Carhampton had won few admirers in this role. The undersecretary at Dublin Castle, Edward Cooke, wrote of him: 'he is so flighty that he alarms the country and harasses the troops dreadfully and it is impossible to do business with him. He is going to England of his own desire and I hope he will be kept there.'[54] In January 1797, Cooke again wrote of him, this time to the chief secretary Thomas Pelham, 'he has different opinions about the defences of Ireland and the conduct of war from every officer in the whole army'.[55] His turbulent spell as commander-in-chief was ended when Sir Ralph Abercromby acceded to the role in his place. His uncompromising and brutal actions during this time were surely a primary motivation behind the attempt on his life and this incident provides an ominous and telling sign of things to come within the parish.

The Farmers' Society for the union of Castleknock first met on 27 November 1797 with the chief secretary of Ireland in the chair. Pelham had ascended to the role of chief secretary in March 1795 and much was expected of him. Unfortunately, his ill health meant that he was frequently absent from office. Similar in composition to the Association for the Protection of Private Property, the chief aims of the Farmers' Society were 'the improvement of agriculture, [and] the encouraging and rewarding [of] faithful, industrious and sober servants and labourers'.[56] During the first meeting of the society, Alexander Kirkpatrick was elected treasurer and Matthew Weld was nominated as secretary. Also present on that day were Robert Wynne, William Kirkpatrick, the Revd David Bricketh, Revd George O'Connor, Francis McFarland, Francis McFarland Jnr, Henry McFarland and Thomas and William Blair. The Longfield map surveying the lands of George Vesey in Westmanstown also apportions part of the land opposite McFarland's holding to a Mr Blair. James and Thomas Blair were also members of the Association for the Protection of Private Property, each paying the standard subscription of £5 13s. 9d.[57] A large iron mill on the banks of the River Liffey in Lucan was the property of William Blair, as his will of 17 October 1833 testifies.[58] This iron mill, described as 'extensive' by Musgrave,[59] is listed in Lieutenant Joseph Archer's 1801 statistical survey of Co. Dublin as comprising eight functioning wheels, over double that of Stokes & Co. of Clonskeagh, the second largest iron mill in Dublin.[60] A standard subscription of £2. 5s. 6d. was required for membership of this society and that same amount was requested from Pelham, Carhampton, Wynne, Kirkpatrick, the Blairs and Francis McFarland. A lesser rate of £1. 2s. 9d. was requested from the younger McFarlands, the clergy and, interestingly, Walter Troy.

Before they were part-time soldiers or church accountants these people were farmers. First and foremost, they earned their very existence from the land they lived on and the significance of this fact cannot be overlooked when the harsh, unpredictable and violent world they lived in is taken into consideration. Survival was still the primary motivation which drove many of them and the consequences of failure were severe in the extreme. As such, their function in life became the key to this survival and, among themselves, this fact was recognized by the importance they attached to the livelihood which they shared and which brought them together. A passage which was transcribed onto the opening page of the Farmers' Society minute book perhaps best illustrates this point. It reads:

> At an annual festival celebrated in Persia, the king dined in public and the chief farmers had the honour of sitting at the table with him when he addressed them in words to this effect. I am one of you, and my subsistence and that of my people rests on the labours of your hands, the succession of the race of man depends on the plough and without you we cannot exist, but your dependence on me is reciprocal, we ought therefore to be brothers and live in perpetual harmony.[61]

Events in Clonsilla during the 1790s are indicative of acute social tension within the locality and were similar to those being experienced across the whole of Ireland. That Henry Lawes Luttrell's ancestral residence was within the parish would appear to be the single defining factor which influenced those events. Owing to Luttrell's power, reputation and past actions, it is highly conceivable that local tenant's apparent compliance with local power structures masked a deep-rooted hatred of their landlord. The area was prone to immediate explosions of orchestrated violence, such as the plan of assassination designed against Luttrell and the murder of Patrick McCormick. That a violent sedition, barely detectable to the local gentry, was spreading amongst the tenants throughout the decade is unquestionable. The organization of the local gentry into associations and societies indicated a desire on their part to protect their position and address the issues which they believed may have placed it under threat. The social separation of landlord and tenant can be measured by the relative inadequacy of these measures to address such grievances, improve security within the locality or achieve any of their social goals.

2. Local experience of the 1798 Rebellion

This chapter covers the tumultuous period of January to December 1798 from the perspective of Clonsilla and its inhabitants, investigating the effect the rebellion had on the area and the actions of key local figures upon the outbreak of the insurrection. An analysis of these facts and reactions to the revolt should provide a telling insight into the values, beliefs and convictions of the wider community of Clonsilla at that time.

During a meeting of the Farmers' Society on 15 January 1798, it was decided that Robert Wynne would head a committee to address the issue of outstanding subscriptions. The same problem that dogged the Association for the Protection of Private Property evidently carried over to this organization as this is a recurring issue during the early meetings of the society. A sense of how the ascendancy mind operated at local level could be obtained through an examination of how the Association dealt with the unfortunate case of the widow Tiernan. The distinct detachment from the injured party reflected the social reality at that time, and by the same token, governmental policy of appeasing calls for radical reform of the political structure by addressing legitimate social grievances is translated to the local context through the initiatives of the Farmers' Society. At a meeting on 29 January 1798 the members present pledged to 'take into consideration the price of labour and of provision in this union and examine whether … the sober and industrious labourer [is able to] procure for himself and family such a comfortable subsistence as we think all such labourers justly entitled.'[1] It was also resolved to establish a village shop in the area, to be 'furnished with such articles as are generally made use of by labourers, manufacturers … To be under the inspection and subject to the regulation of this society.' This measure would have suited the dual purpose of ensuring that labourers and tenants were adequately provided for, thus ensuring social cohesion and improving the attitude of the labourers towards the propertied, and also in reaffirming the control and the hold of the members over the local community. Incentives for labourers to carry out their work in the most efficient and effective manner were also provided for, as these 'rewards for excellence in husbandry' testify.

The best ploughman with oxen	£2 5s. 6d.
The best ploughman with horses	£2 5s. 6d.

The labourer who shall appear to have brought up the
greatest number of legitimate children in habits of
industry to the age of twelve years £2 5s. 6d.

The labourer who has given the greatest number of
years service £2 5s. 6d.

The dairy maid who has given the greatest number of
years service £1 2s. 9d.

To three boys and three girls under the age of twelve ...
to have earned the most money in the year in country
business £3 0s. 3d.

To six boys and six girls at school in Castleknock,
Blanchardstown and Porterstown as most attentive
to learning and best behaved. £3 0s. 3d.[2]

Robert Wynne, Alexander Kirkpatrick, David Bricketh and Walter Troy were appointed as inspectors for Clonsilla and it was also decided to present a medal to the farmer 'who has most comfortable habitation for his labourers'. On 10 February 1798, the Dublin Agricultural Society accepted a proposal to become a corresponding society to that of Castleknock by expressing their 'great satisfaction of hearing of the commencement of an institution so likely to become highly useful to farmers in general'. As a goodwill gesture they forwarded several essays and hints on agriculture and farming written by Sir John Sinclair, president of the Agricultural Board in London, for the perusal of the Castleknock members.[3]

The practice of using oxen for the purpose of ploughing fields, the best practitioner of which received £2. 5s. 6d. under the 'rewards for excellence in husbandry' scheme, was an example of the contemporary and innovative farming methods that were adopted and encouraged by the agricultural society in Castleknock. While horses continued to be the animal most commonly used for this purpose, Lieutenant Joseph Archer reported in his 1801 statistical survey of the county of Dublin that 'many of the best farmers work oxen tolerably well appointed, in traces, with a collar etc'.[4] Archer believed that oxen were advantageous compared to horses for several reasons. He specifically stated that they were 'well adapted to all solid heavy draughts, generally reckoned to fatten better after moderate labour for a year or two and cheaper than horses (of about three to two)'. Another significant advantage that the use of oxen entailed was in their suitability for work, if 'an accident should befall any of their limbs' and 'render them useless for labour'. A horse, in the same circumstances, served no purpose, whereas oxen may then be stall fed. Archer advised any farmers aspiring to employ these methods that 'a bit in their [oxen] mouth, the same as a horse's, would make them more manageable and the ploughman can then, with long reins, guide them as he pleases.'[5]

Early in February 1798, martial law was proclaimed in eight Kildare baronies and two baronies further south in Co. Cork. While the sentiments of rebellion were bubbling under the surface, governmental and United Irish leadership engaged in a strategic posturing of sorts. They each wished to display the full extent of their capabilities while paradoxically aiming to maintain an element of surprise. In this climate a Tyrone magistrate, Thomas Knox, declared that 'the first up will carry the day'.[6] On 26 February, the United Irishmen claimed 110,990 men for Ulster and 100,634 for Munster. For the four provinces of Ireland, a total of 279,896 was claimed by the organization.[7] On 12 March, a major propaganda coup was achieved by Dublin Castle with the arrest of the Leinster committee of the United Irishmen at Oliver Bond's house in Dublin. Among those arrested was George Cummins, a Kildare apothecary and representative for that county on the committee.

In late 1797, John Pollock, a clerk of the town of Kildare, gave an account to the town assizes, recommending that more troops be committed for its defence. He described Cummins as 'the agent and confidential friend of Lord Edward [Fitzgerald]' and stated that he 'appeared [to be] the executive officer of sedition and rebellion'.[8] Pollock had also affirmed that Cummins had acted as treasurer for the United Irishmen and employed and paid solicitors and council for the United Irish prisoners.[9] A description of events surrounding the arrests at Oliver Bond's house which appeared in the *Dublin Evening Post* on 19 July 1798 describes Cummins as having been of 'thin countenance, rather tall with dark lank hair'. By association, he would also have been involved in the practice of packing juries with sympathetic or intimidated citizens during trials of United Irishmen, an effective tactic which frustrated the Castle's legal suppression of the organization. In a letter to under secretary, Edward Cooke, John Wolfe of Balbriggan described the murder of Patrick Nicholson at Rathbridge on the Curragh in November 1797. Nicholson had been responsible for Cummins having been previously lodged in gaol. In order to intimidate Nicholson, 'his house was burned, but he received damages from the grand jury and so it was necessary for him to be murdered'. In traditional Defender fashion, 'a number of savages, with their faces blackened and shirts over their coats ... butchered him with more than savage barbarity'.[10] After his arrest at Bond's house, Cummins denied all knowledge of and connections with the United Irishmen; he was even so brazen to suggest that he had found himself in Bond's house after following his clerk into the premises on a whim.[11] After his interrogation, the exasperated magistrate concluded his report by writing, 'being obstinate in denying everything, he was committed.'[12] While the Castle had succeeded in putting many important leaders behind bars, planning for the rebellion had not ceased and by April 1798 the replacement Leinster provincial had issued a set of instructions essentially designed to prepare the organization for rebellion.[13]

A meeting of the Farmers' Society on 26 March 1798 postponed consider-ations of labour, provisions and village shops indefinitely. Effectively, the society's humanitarian mission was suspended. The organizing of a ploughing match, to be held in Walter Troy's field in June of that year, indicated a desire not to allow the situation spoil all plans for society business and social interaction. It also provides further evidence of the healthy competitive spirit which existed among members, which they, in turn, attempted to foster within the labouring class through the promise of substantial rewards for exceptional agricultural output and performance. The Association for the Protection of Private Property was not meeting at this time, although it is likely that their affairs and concerns were being addressed during yeomanry business, given the nature of that body and the senior personnel involved.

On 2 April, owing to his deteriorating health, Thomas Pelham, a member of the Society, was replaced as chief secretary in Dublin Castle by Lord Castlereagh. Five days later, the final meeting of the Farmers' Society prior to the outbreak of rebellion (headlined 'special meeting' in the minute book) empowered Alexander Kirkpatrick 'to lay out as much of the premium fund as can be spared … in laying the new materials for the spinners of woollen and yarn'.[14] This indicates a pragmatic approach to a local humanitarian or economic concern and a will to ensure that a sense of forward-looking momentum was maintained during any civil uprising or attack on the existing social structures and way of life. As the month drew to a close, Lieutenant General Gerard Lake succeeded Sir Ralph Abercromby as commander-in-chief of the armed forces of the crown in Ireland.

Lord Edward FitzGerald was arrested on 19 May 1798, after a ferocious struggle in which one of his captors, a yeomanry captain, Daniel Ryan, was fatally wounded. Another, magistrate William Swan, was also wounded but eventually recovered. FitzGerald's resistance ceased only when Major Henry Charles Sirr, head of the Dublin police, entered the scene and fired an incapacitating pistol shot in his direction. One week previously, on 12 May, a notice had been published in the *Freeman's Journal* declaring a reward of £1,000 for the capture of Lord Edward.[15] As a national figurehead, symbolic leader and one of few United Irishmen with any real military experience, his capture marked a bitter blow for the rebellion's chances of success.

The capture of FitzGerald also marked the high point of Francis Higgins' career as Castle gossip gatherer. In November 1797, he had succeeded in procuring, as an informer, the services of Francis Magan, a young barrister who held a modest position in the Dublin United Irishmen. After FitzGerald's escape from Oliver Bond's house, Magan had kept Higgins continually informed of FitzGerald's whereabouts, and also of his 'watches and spies, armed, who give an account of danger being near'. On 18 May, by a stroke of good fortune, Magan himself was asked to conceal Lord Edward in his own house in Ussher's Island, 'disguised – he wears a wig, or may be otherwise metamorphosed'.[16] After an exchange of pistol fire with Sirr and his arresting party, Lord Edward narrowly escaped on that occasion. His location was again betrayed the following night by Magan, allowing Higgins to collect the £1,000 reward offered on 12 May. It would appear that Higgins never paid any of this money over to Magan, and the Castle were forced to make him an *ex gratia* payment some years later.[17] Thomas Magan, father of Francis, had been a long-time friend of Higgins and had died in 1797, apparently owing him some money. Magan also appears to have had a connection to the earl of Carhampton, 'to whom his father [Thomas] and self owed obligation respecting a lease granted by his lordship'.[18]

At six o'clock on the morning of Thursday, 24 May 1798, Robert Wynne was informed by two of his yeomanry corps of an armed rebel attack on the neighbouring village of Dunboyne. A considerable number of rebels had entered the town and attacked the local police house, where it was alleged that they murdered three Protestant constables and spared an equal number of Catholics. A Mr Creighton, a Protestant revenue officer, was also said to have fallen victim to the rebels. The local vicar, the Revd Duncan, was believed to have fled in time but his house was attacked and stripped of valuables to the value of £500. Upon hearing of the outbreak of rebellion, Wynne proceeded to the County Meath village of Ratoath, less than ten kilometres from Clonsilla, with four of his own cavalry and 11 regular Angus Highlanders, commanded by George Armstrong of the artillery. The group was said to have been reinforced by Frederick Falkiner and 18 of the 5th Dragoons.[19] In Ratoath, the rebels had captured Captain Hamilton George, MP for Co. Meath, Elias Corbally, lieutenant of the yeomanry corps which George commanded, and several privates of that corps. When Wynne and his rescue party arrived in the village, the rebels were on the point of hanging their captives. Wynne led two successful cavalry charges, killing 35 rebels and forcing the rest to flee.

Later that morning, a private from George's Ratoath cavalry arrived in Navan and informed John Preston of the attacks in Dunboyne, a similar occurrence in the town of Dunshaughlin and of their own lucky escape in Ratoath.[20] Given the direction of the main route between Co. Meath and Dublin city, Navan was assumed to be the next port of call for the rebels. After their successful rescue attempt, Wynne's party returned for home without the 18 Dragoons who had reinforced them. In the meantime, the dispersed rebels had regrouped and must have observed the diminution of Loyalist numbers. Determined for revenge, they pursued the returning party as far as Clonee Bridge, located on the then main Dublin–Navan road and a little over one kilometre from Clonsilla, where six of the Highlanders under Lieutenant Armstrong were said to have been killed halting the progress of the rebels.[21]

On that same day in Clonee, the rebels were said to have intercepted another detachment of Fencibles, killed a number of them, taken some prisoner and stolen all of their baggage.[22] The *Freeman's Journal* of the following day reported: 'yesterday, two companies of the Rea Fencibles arrived in town [Dublin] after a fatiguing march. They came from Belfast, but last from Clonee, near Dunsaughlin, in which neighbourhood they were surprised by a considerable number of insurgents, and all their baggage taken from them'.[23]

Later that morning, Thomas Connor and Thomas Atkinson of Dunboyne entered the house of James Brassington of Ballymacarney at Kilbride, backed by a considerable party of United Irish rebels. Brassington held the position of warden in Dunboyne Protestant church.[24] At the court martial of the two men, this party was claimed by Brassington to be in the region of about 'thirty or forty others, all of whom were armed'.[25] Brassington also claimed that they spent about half an hour in the house that morning, during which time he heard Connor boast of how he burned Dunboyne police house, murdered the policemen, killed some Highlanders and stole some of their baggage. He stated that Atkinson then threatened to burn his house down but left without doing so, only to return, oddly, and invite Brassington to join them. The rebel party was claimed to have taken a sword, a blunderbuss, a musket, a pistol, some balls and four horses from the house. He then concluded his evidence by saying that he had known Connor for 16 years and Atkinson for three or four, and specified that the two were ringleaders on that morning.

During the court martial, Richard Brassington, brother of James, corroborated what had been said, and also identified Connor as the principal leader of the two, wearing 'a white jacket with green facings'.[26] The testimony of Patrick Condron, rebel and former servant to the Brassingtons, who was captured by the lawyer's cavalry and interrogated at the royal exchange in Dublin, describes the rebel commander as having been 'dressed in white faced with green'. The commander appeared to be unknown to Condron, who also 'heard that he was in the Kildare militia'. Given the proximity of Kilbride to Dunboyne and the nature of the rural community which resided in that area, it is unlikely that Condron would not have recognized Connor as the commander on that morning. This casts some doubt over the legitimacy of Brassington's testimony but also raises questions over Condron's honesty. Atkinson and Connor were later sentenced to death for their part in that morning's events. Jane Connor, wife of Thomas, made a final plea for mercy for her husband at his court martial, claiming that they were sleeping upon the outbreak of the rebellion and he was induced from his bed by a large group of men. She was unsuccessful, however, despite the evidence of several corroborating witnesses.[27] After the rebellion, the Brassingtons were never to return to Ballymacarney, as it was believed locally that they had perjured themselves at the trial, and they justifiably feared retribution as a result.[28]

Equally, they may have been killed simply in revenge for their indicting statements, be they perjured or not.

In the opinion of Liam Chambers, 'the fundamental purpose of the United Irish rebellion of 1798 was the overthrow of the Irish administration in Dublin; hence their primary military objective was the capture of the capital'.[29] Thomas Graham, in his work *Dublin in 1798,* illustrates that a three-phase insurgency plan gradually emerged to achieve this aim. The first part of this plan involved the capture of key sites in Dublin. Effective government suppression in the metropolis seriously hampered this integral first step of rebellion – not only had Lord Edward been arrested, but so too had the Sheares brothers, Henry and John. John had assumed command of the United Irish organization after the arrest of the Leinster Directory at Bond's house. Samuel Neilson, who had been editor of the Belfast-published United Irish newspaper *Northern Star,* issued the orders for rebels to mobilize just hours before he himself was arrested, on 23 May, while attempting to rescue Lord Edward. Also, Dublin Castle's effective spy network ensured that their intelligence information was reliable, allowing them to occupy projected rebel points of assembly upon the outbreak of insurrection, forcing the would-be insurgents to disengage and quietly return home.[30] The stopping of the mail coaches in Dublin was to be the signal for a general uprising in more outlying areas, their non-arrival in those various districts would be an indication to local United Irishmen that the uprising had begun.

The second phase of the military plan involved the region immediately outside the capital. Higgins had informed the Castle that this 'involved the rebel occupation of positions from Garretstown, Naul ... and Dunboyne and circuitously round the metropolis to Dunleary'.[31] The clear intention of this phase of the plan was to ensure that reinforcements arriving from other parts of the country would be engaged with rebels in these outlying areas for a long enough time in order to allow the rebellion within the capital to take hold. The next phase of the plan was less clearly defined but was to involve rebels in the remaining counties engaging the military presence in their own localities, further hampering attempts to reinforce Dublin militarily and preventing the second layer of rebel mobilization from coming under attack.

At around 11 o'clock on the night of Friday, 25 May, George Cummins led a party of rebels in an attack on the extensive iron works of a Mr Blair at Lucan, located on the site of the present Hills Industrial Estate about one hundred metres from the bridge over the river Liffey into the village. Cummins, said to be a Catholic member of the Clonsilla yeomanry corps, had defected upon the outbreak of the rebellion despite having taken an oath of allegiance to the king.[32] The raiding party which he now led, said to number up to 100 men, entered the iron works variously armed with guns, pikes and sticks and demanded the key to Blair's office.[33]

The Mr Blair in question, most likely William Blair, was from a prominent local family, many of whom, like him, were members of the Association for the Protection of Private Property and also of the Farmers' Society of Castleknock. As the owner of a large local iron mill of eight wheels and an acquaintance of the local yeomanry commanders, it is conceivable that Blair had received commissions or requests from them to manufacture the weapons and munitions necessary to effectively arm the new local defence corps, a measure which had met with some opposition from the somewhat marginalized Walter Troy. In comparison to the paltry number of four privates who had sprung to Wynne's aid upon the outbreak of rebellion, the substantial force who walked to Lucan under Cummins' command suggests that there may have been some credence behind Troy's objections to arm the locals, other than to compensate for his own wounded pride. Cummins had clearly been informed of where to find the arms which he sought and many of Blair's workmen joined his raiding party after the attack. They were reported to have declared their intention to march to Dunboyne and meet 'the others', before advancing to the rebel camp now forming at the hill of Tara. The evidence would suggest that on this occasion Wynne had acted rashly, allowing his own ambition, objectives and tenacity to cloud his judgment to such an extent that he made what had proved to be a rare occurrence in his life, a serious and very public error of judgment.

A private from Captain George's Ratoath cavalry had immediately set out to inform John Preston of the Navan militia of their own narrow escape from rebel hands on the morning of Thursday, 24 May. Suitably anxious that Navan appeared to be the next logical point of rebel attack, Preston wrote to the commanding officer of Kells for reinforcements. A reconnoitring unit made up from numbers from both corps soon reported that Co. Meath was in a general state of insurrection. Preston was also made aware that the regiment of Rea Fencibles were then on a march from Belfast to Dublin as reinforcements for the capital. Preston intercepted this body and it was agreed with their commander, Captain Scobie, that a detachment of Fencibles would join up with local yeomanry units in Navan and launch an attack on Dunshaughlin, a United Irish rallying point in rebel hands. The Fencibles arrived in Navan on the night of 25 May, the same night as the attack on the iron mill at Lucan.[34] Unaware of the rebel camp now forming on the hill of Tara, the joint units marched on Dunshaughlin to find it completely deserted. Scobie is said to have steadfastly refused to stay in the county any longer, at which point Preston informed him that he would personally ride to Dublin and obtain orders from the lord lieutenant commanding him to do so. As a compromise, Scobie left Preston three companies, a battalion cannon and a promise to return. In a letter written a few days later, Scobie names Captain McLean as commander of the unit that marched on to Tara later that day as reports began to circulate about the huge rebel presence now forming there.

The Hill of Tara may have seemed an ideal rallying point for United Irish rebels, both symbolically and strategically. It provided a commanding view of the surrounding countryside and was well situated for cutting off the Dublin–Navan road, a likely route for reinforcements. In addition to the ancient earthen fortifications which provided defensive cover at its base, the hill itself was strongly identified in Irish folklore as a symbol of independence by having been the ancient seat of the Irish high king. The rebels, who were assembling there over a period of three days and were reputed to have numbered up to 5,000, were said to be in high spirits due to a perceived Loyalist reluctance to attack them. At the point of bayonet, the Fencibles who had been captured at Clonee were forced to instruct the rebels in the use of the captured arms. Three pairs of green colours had been set up and 40 camp fires were providing boiled mutton and other food. The 25 May edition of the *Freeman's Journal* reported that the house of Samuel Garnett had been attacked near Clonee and that 125 of his sheep taken away.[35] Garnett was James Brassington's fellow church warden at Dunboyne.[36]

The rebels would have been relatively well armed after the capture of Fencible arms and the successful attack on the iron works in Lucan. However, organization was poor, the rebels were unsure of what to do next and discipline was said to have been non existent. On Saturday morning, just before Loyalist forces converged on the site, three horse loads of whiskey in barrels was said to have been seized by the rebels, who proceeded to get drunk in spite of their leader's orders. It has been suggested that Lord Fingall, whose cavalry unit fought at Tara, had paid a Navan distiller by the name of Cregan to send the cargo past the rebel camp.[37] Captain Blanche of the Fencibles wrote an account of the battle from the army's perspective, describing how as the Loyalist force approached, the rebels 'put their hats on top of their pikes, sent forth some dreadful yells and at the same time beginning to jump and put themselves in various singular attitudes, as if bidding defiance'. The rebel commander, identified by his green and white uniform, also came forward and made a 'very pompous salute' before returning with 'great precipitation'.[38]

The infantry then advanced to within 50 yards of the insurgents and opened fire, the cavalry deployed on the left and right to prevent the rebels from outflanking them. As confusion, eagerness to fight and drunkenness reigned within the camp, the rebels made a fatal mistake early in the day by abandoning their strong position and charging down the hill. Initially, the Loyalist infantry ran as they were unable to get near the rebels behind the eight to ten foot long pikes, but as the infantry were fleeing downhill, the Loyalist cavalry charged. On the wide open ground the horses of the cavalry were able to charge, wheel and charge again, their swords hacking at the confused rebels. The final decisive blow, in terms of rebel chances of victory, occurred when the canon began to open fire and the rebels scattered.

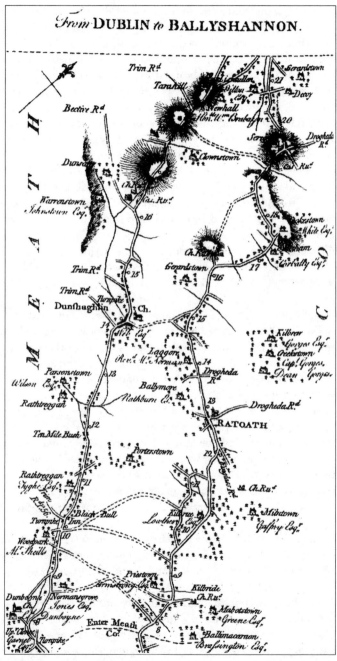

5 The likely route of Clonsilla rebels to the Hill of Tara via Dunboyne,
Dunshaughlin and Ratoath. Taylor and Skinner, *Map of the roads of Ireland* (1783).

While the fighting continued, from this point there was never any doubt as to the outcome of the battle. As fighting raged on, rebel strategy seemed to focus on capturing the canon, a tactic that was without success. Of the latter moments of the battle, Blanche wrote 'and finding the men's ammunition almost expended, and our situation getting still more critical, I found it absolutely necessary to make one decisive effort which was gallantly executed by grenadiers'.[39] The grenadiers, who were the men of the greatest height and strength of each regiment and most effective for close combat fighting, captured the last rebel stronghold at the graveyard with a bayonet charge. As a final act of defiance, the rebels made one more desperate attempt for the canon and almost succeeded in surrounding it before, as Blanche described, 'the officer who commanded the gun, having laid the match to it, before they could completely surround it, prostrated ten or twelve of the assailants and dispersed the remainder … Returning their invasion and crowned our operations with a complete victory'.[40]

The *Freeman's Journal* of 29 May printed a letter written by Captain Scobie of the Rea Fencibles to Lieutenant General Lake, informing him of his account of the comprehensive Loyalist victory at Tara. It reads:

> The division, consisting of five companies of his Majesty's Rea regiment of Fencible infantry arrived here yesterday, accompanied by Lord Fingall's troop of yeomen cavalry, Captain Preston's troop of cavalry, lower Kells ditto and Captain Molloy's troop of yeomanry infantry. At 3.30 p.m. I was informed that a considerable force of the rebel insurgents had taken station on the Tara Hill. I instantly detached three companies of our division with one field piece, and the above corps of yeomanry, to the spot, under the command of Captain Mc Lean of the Reas. The rebels fled in all directions, three hundred and fifty were found dead on the field this morning, among whom is their commander, in full uniform – many more were killed and wounded. Our loss is inconsiderable, being nine rank and file killed, sixteen rank and file wounded.
>
> (dated Dunshaughlin, Sunday morning, 27 May 1798)[41]

Also on that day, the lord lieutenant, Earl Camden, wrote to the duke of Portland, secretary of state and Whig cabinet member in charge of Irish affairs, and provided a similar narrative of the day's events. His letter stated:

> I have the satisfaction to inform your grace that the body of rebels, who for some days had been in considerable force to the northward of Dublin, were yesterday defeated, with very great loss on their part, by a party of the Rea Fencibles, and the neighbouring yeomanry corps, on the Hill of Tara. Five companies of the Rea Fencibles, under the

command of Captain Scobie, had halted yesterday at Dunshaughlin on their march to Dublin; and hearing that the rebels were in great force, and had taken station on Tara Hill, Captain Scobie detached three of his companies, under the command of Captain McLean, with one field piece to the spot.[42]

It would appear that Scobie successfully concealed his initial reluctance to follow John Preston's advice from the official account of events, ensuring that the credit for the overwhelming victory was attributed to his own astute command and military capabilities.

Elsewhere in Ireland, rebel fortunes were not greatly dissimilar to those witnessed on the Hill of Tara. The intended plan for rebellion centred on the raising of an insurgency within the metropolis of Dublin, so failing that, the actual rebellion as it occurred made little military sense. Letters conveyed out of Kilmainham jail suggest that a number of insurgents who should have rallied had not done so and that those who did were poorly organized and inadequately commanded. Higgins wrote on Friday, 25 May:

> There has been letters conveyed out of Kilmainham Jail and at Humphrey's at Usher's Quay … in which complaints were made that their sworn friends beyond Drogheda and in the county of Louth had shamefully kept back! – that if the United force from Dunleary [had gone] round the mountains, bringing forward part of the Wicklow men, and obtaining the Meath and Dunboyne numbers to act with them by Whitsun Monday [28 May], 'Ireland would still be saved'.[43]

These sentiments only further highlight the effectiveness of the Castle's pre-rebellion campaign of arrests and intelligence gathering while emphasizing the frustration of the United Irish leadership at their incarceration and inept second line of command.

The court martial of George Cummins took place in the barracks of Dublin on 11 July 1798. Also charged on that day were Thomas Connor and Thomas Atkinson of Dunboyne. Cummins himself was charged with being:

> principally concerned with a party of the rebels in an attack on Mr Blair's works at Lucan … and of carrying off a considerable number of arms and ammunition and several of the artificers in said works and having afterwards joined the rebels at Tara Hill and fought there against the King's troops, he having been heretofore a yeoman in the Clonsilla Cavalry and taken the oath of allegiance.[44]

Francis McFarland Jnr was the first witness to be sworn and he identified Cummins as a former member of the Clonsilla cavalry. The 1796 maps surveying the lands of Captain George Vesey in Westmanstown attributed a significant land holding to the McFarlands, adjacent to the earl of Carhampton's Luttrellstown demesne.[45] Contemporary maps illustrate that the route between Clonsilla and Lucan is unchanged from that of today, and as such, Cummins would have passed the McFarlands' land on the way from Clonsilla or Dunboyne to Lucan.

The next witness to be sworn was John Lyons, a workman at the iron mill. He identified Cummins as having entered the mill carrying a sword and demanding arms before making him a prisoner, along with several of Blair's workmen, and marching them towards Dunboyne. He also conclusively stated that many of the men who entered the yard empty handed left well armed. While being marched to Dunboyne, Lyons was said to have overheard 'several of the party say that they were going to the battle of Tara'. Lyons' answers are short, precise and damning. An examination of the transcript of the court martial indicates that it is highly likely that Lyons was well coached and prompted prior to his testimony. The name of Lyons was previously noted in the area through John Lyons, the former clerk of Clonsilla church who died in 1792 and was survived by his wife and young child, a minor, whose name was not recorded on parish registers.[46]

After Lyons' evidence, James Carroll took the stand and provided an identical testimony which incriminated Cummins as the ring leader on the night of 24 May. When questioning Carroll himself, Cummins disputed the statement that he entered the iron mill with any arms. Carroll seems to have conceded eventually on this point, only to reiterate the fact that he certainly mounted the hill back to Dunboyne with a gun which he had procured from the yard. John Lunders, a 14-year-old boy, testified that he was brought to the battle at the Tara Hill by Cummins, who was armed with a pistol. He also stated that he had known Cummins for between two and three years.

The prosecution having made their case, Cummins was called to make the case for the defence. In response to the question 'what is the general character of John Lyons?' Captain John Rickey stated: 'I do not think that John Lyons is a man deserving credit on his oath'. This being the only recorded testimony of Captain Rickey, the transcript abruptly ends 'the pris[oner] here closed his defence', but not before the scribe noted and hastily crossed out what clearly states 'W[illia]m Blair sworn'. What cannot be concluded was whether Blair had the opportunity to be cross-examined by Cummins or if the nature of that testimony was deemed unsuitable for inclusion by the court martial scribe. Regardless, Cummins was sentenced to death and the area commander, Lieutenant-General Craig, was ordered to make the necessary arrangements for the execution.[47]

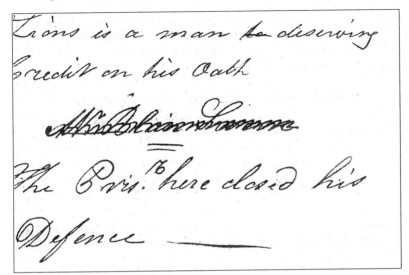

6 Transcripts of the court martial of George Cummins, erasing
Mr Blair's testimony from the record.

After the convictions of Cummins, Atkinson and Connor, a large number
of United Irish rebels met in Dunboyne on the night of 11 July 1798. Higgins
reported to Dublin Castle:

> On Wednesday [11 July], Power, one of the people I have long retained
> and received intelligence from, went with two others to Dunboyne and
> was at the meeting of a large body of rebels there on that night. They
> consisted of some thousands, where the question of rescuing Bond,
> Jackson etc. was agitated and they declared (those who acted as officers)
> 'that were they supplied with ammunition as promised, they would risk
> everything; but being deceived in that point, they could not until such
> was obtained for them, and Bond had in his hands many thousands
> accounted for'. Power says there was cavalry among them, as well
> mounted and armed as any in the city, that wore green uniform.[48]

While not hinted at by Higgins, the fact that the timing of the meeting
coincided with the convictions of local United Irishmen must surely have
instigated calls for a rescue attempt. The finality of the sentences handed down
would have contributed to the feeling amongst sympathizers that immediate
and decisive action was necessary. Despite the effective counter intelligence,
suppression of insurrection and conviction of captured rebels, such meetings

must surely have served as a dangerous reminder to the Castle authorities that a determined and well-supported enemy still lurked among them, waiting for an ideal opportunity to exact revenge upon the propertied and privileged. Higgins further stated:

> a considerable number of the infantry (or foot) were ragged, forlorn poor devils, armed with scythes, pitchforks, pikes, muskets, etc. Some of the officers are tradesmen from the city who boast that an immediate supply would be had from France, that people from all quarters flocked to their standard. Their body when fully assembled was 18,000 and the detached party's that would be collected in twenty four hours would be more than 80,000 through Kildare, Wicklow, etc., etc … Their emissaries induce the wretched, misguided people of the country to unite in their infernal plan, they have in every part held out the lure of plunder, and that the city of Dublin, with all its spoils and riches would be theirs in a few days.[49]

Transcripts of a letter conveyed out of the lord lieutenant's office on 14 July 1798 to General Meyrick 'acknowledge the receipt of your two letters sent by express to Lieutenant General Craig and communicate his Excellency's appreciation of the execution and decision with which you have acted against the rebels in county Meath.'[50] Five days later, a letter sent to General Craig from the same office listed several recent courts martial, including that of Cummins, and casts some doubt over the legitimacy of the sentences passed down by them. It reads:

> The Lord Lieutenant, having taken into due consideration proceedings of several court martials and having observed that those who have been convicted of charges alleged against them have been sentenced to death or to transportation for life directs me to acquaint you that, in his opinion, most, if not all, of the above cases will admit of mitigation. His Excellency is further of the opinion, on consideration of the enormous expense and inconvenience attending such transportation, that it would be more conducive that the sentences should be commuted to service for life, wherever His Majesty shall be pleased to direct, should the persons convicted appear, upon examination by a staff surgeon, to be fit for such service.

The cases of Thomas Connor and Thomas Atkinson, it was reported, remained for further consideration. On 27 July, another letter dispatched to General Craig informed him that

The lord lieutenant, having taken into mature consideration the proceedings of the court martial of Thomas Atkinson and Thomas Connor, is pleased to approve of the sentence passed upon them and desires you will direct the same to be carried into execution at the place where the offence was committed.[51]

The cases of Cummins, Atkinson and Connor are indicative of Cornwallis's decided government policy of severity and compassion. Lord Charles Cornwallis, often remembered as the British general who surrendered the North American colonies to George Washington, had succeeded the earl of Camden as viceroy on 20 June 1798. In most instances, rebel leaders were severely dealt with while their misguided followers were allowed a considerable measure of leniency, after they surrendered their weapons and subjugated to an oath of loyalty to the crown. These examples illustrate the fine line which potentially existed between those terms of reference, and the misfortune of those people who found themselves on the wrong side of the policy.

A meeting of the Association for the Protection of Private Property, chaired by Francis McFarland, took place on 30 October at the Royal Exchange in Dublin. Indicative of the change in local power structures that the rebellion would instigate, Robert Wynne formally resigned as secretary and Thomas Blair was appointed in his place. Prior to the attack on the iron works in May, the Blairs played little or no active role in the Association. Despite having paid the original subscription in 1792, they were only recorded as having attended one subsequent meeting, on 13 September of that year. McFarland noted that Alexander Kirkpatrick retained his role as treasurer before stating that the meeting was 'too thinly attended to enter into business.'[52]

A meeting on 5 November 1798 provided evidence of continuing disturbances within the area, as a reward of £50 was offered following 'the many robberies and murders [that] have been lately committed in different parts of these districts by an armed banditti'. The problem of armed banditti was experienced, to various extents, across Ireland in the months and years following the rebellion. Refusing to accept that their cause was lost, they were a constant scourge to government and a substantial threat to local security. By the end of the year, the process of socially excluding those involved in the rebellion and the subsequent disturbances had already begun. During a meeting of the Farmers' Society, it was 'resolved that who shall appear to the society to have been concerned in the rebellion or in any further disturbances of the county shall never receive any of the premiums offered by this society'.[53] A copy of a letter sent by Society member and former Chief Secretary Thomas Pelham, dated Stanmer, 3 December 1798, is transcribed into the Society minute book. It reads:

Although the state of my health has made it necessary for me to relinquish my situation as chief secretary and I cannot expect to attend your agricultural meetings at Castleknock, I hope you will allow me to remain a member of that society and to remit my annual subscription. I fear that the disturbances have prevented any meeting this summer, but I hope not. – You will persist in your plan and if I can be of use in collecting information or otherwise you may command me.[54]

There is circumstantial evidence to suggest that the George Cummins who led the attack on the iron works in Lucan was the same man as had occupied a prominent position on the Leinster committee of the United Irishmen. Cummins, the Kildare apothecary, whom John Pollock had described as 'the agent and confidential friend of Lord Edward',[55] could well have specifically targeted the Clonsilla yeomanry as a corps likely to be susceptible to seditious intentions. His menacing presence at the Kildare assizes and role in 'packing' juries with sympathetic or intimidated jurors suggests that he had a natural ability in this form of underhand activity. Given the prominence of Lord Carhampton in the locality, outward signs of rebellious intent on a day-to-day basis were likely to have been minimal in the area, however conflicting this was with the reality of the situation. The plan of assassination designed against the Earl did include uniformed members of the local yeomanry and Walter Troy, one of the few prominent Catholics in the local gentry, seems to have been opposed to the arming of his co-religionists from the outset. Feelings against the Luttrells in the area ran so high that, upon the outbreak of rebellion, locals desecrated the vault of Colonel Henry Luttrell (Carhampton's grandfather) in Clonsilla graveyard and smashed his skull with a pickaxe.[56] Shortly after the rebellion, Carhampton was to sell the Luttrellstown demesne, thus ending the families 450 year association with the area.

In the opinion of Liam Chambers, 'the rebels in north Kildare and west Dublin were closely connected, and Lucan was a key United Irish meeting point previous to the outbreak'.[57] Indeed, the Lucan United Irish leader Thomas Lynch, son of a local innkeeper of the same name, was said to have lead the attack on Blair's mill with Cummins.[58] If the Cummins of the Leinster committee had been involved in events from Lucan to Tara, he would have assumed a senior role in that body of rebels, most likely that of overall commander. Patrick Condron stated that the commander who appeared at the Brassingtons' house was said to have been 'dressed in white faced with green', as was the rebel leader at Tara Hill. He had also 'heard that he [the commander] was in the Kildare militia', that being the militia of the town in which Cummins resided.[59]

There is, however, a considerable body of evidence to suggest that there were, in fact, two men of that name who were active during this time. It is important to consider first the court martial of George Cummins, who led the attack on the iron works at Lucan. While it was stated that he was at the engagement at Tara, a claim that the prisoner is not recorded to have disputed, there is no attempt to name him as the commander on that day. Given the sense of partiality tending to a conviction in that case, any reasonable claim that would have secured a successful prosecution and penalty of death being passed on the prisoner would not have been omitted from the evidence. This fact was not lost on the lord lieutenant, who later reviewed the sentence and recommended that it be lessened in line with government policy. The evidence of Richard Brassington at the trials of Connor and Atkinson, which made specific and damning claims on the dress of Connor, namely that he was wearing 'a white jacket with green facings',[60] was enough to ensure that those two prisoners were escorted to within a few kilometres of their homes to be executed. It was unlikely that Connor was in the Kildare militia, given that James Brassington also claimed to have known him for 16 years, but there must have been more credence in the claims that he was an active leader on that day.

The members of the Leinster committee of the United Irishmen, who were arrested at Oliver Bond's, were held in custody during the period of the rebellion. The Kilmainham treaty, signed in 1798, halted the government executions of United Irish leaders in return for confessions and information. George Cummins, it appears, was fortunate to have found himself on the right side of this treaty. Since these prisoners had proved resourceful in communicating with the outside world, Cornwallis instructed that they be sent to Fort George in the Scottish Highlands, near Inverness. On 19 March 1799, they were conveyed there with only a few hours notice and without being told of their final destination.[61] The list of prisoners held in Kilmainham in 1798 clearly stated that George Cummins was arrested on 13 March 1798 for 'treasonable practices' along with the remainder of the Leinster committee. The same registry also records that he was sent to Fort George on 19 March of the following year.[62] It can be conclusively stated, therefore, that George Cummins, 'the agent and confidential friend of Lord Edward',[63] was in government custody when George Cummins, described by Musgrave as a 'popish yeoman of the Clonsilla cavalry',[64] attacked Mr Blair's iron works at Lucan.

When the Fort George prisoners arrived at their destination for a three year and three month detention, the Revd Dr Steele Dickson, a Presbyterian minister, was alarmed to find that government papers had represented the insurrection as a 'popish rebellion'. In order to challenge this perception, which was generally believed in Scotland, he took a note of his 20 fellow prisoners and requested that they list themselves by their religious persuasion. Cummins, who Michael Durey describes as an 'Ulster Apothecary living in Kildare',[65] classed himself as one of six Presbyterians. His fellow prisoners included four Roman Catholics and ten members of the established Church of Ireland.[66]

A distinct sectarian element can be detected when considering events in Clonsilla and surrounding areas in 1798. The targeting of Protestant police officers and clergymen in Dunboyne indicated this, as did the treatment and ultimate vindication of Walter Troy. His previous doubts relating to his co-religionists' desire to bear arms loyally appeared to have been well founded. Troy's Roman Catholic faith is likely to have influenced both his acquisition of such intelligence and the fact that it was not acted upon. While local tenants appear to have participated in the rebellion in large numbers, their organization appears to have been poor and doomed to failure. It is difficult to assess what impact the capture of the national leadership of the United Irishmen would have had upon the organization within the locality. The successful attacks on Blair's iron mill and Samuel Garnett's farm are likely to have been planned long in advance of the rebellion. The actions of rebels in the field of combat indicate a battle plan that was devoid of any military strategy or capability on the day. Despite the overwhelming success of the government forces, however, it was unlikely that local society would continue without change after so violent an upheaval.

Ballymun Library Tel: 8421890

3. Social change and economic recovery after the rebellion

While the United Irish rebellion of 1798 ultimately failed in its attempt to overthrow British authority in Ireland, the power bases and political structures which were in place prior to the insurrection were to be altered in the years that followed it. After the rising, a parliamentary union with Westminster became inevitable. Passed in 1800, the Act of Union is generally accepted as marking the birth of a new era in the history of Irish politics. In the opinion of R.F. Foster, however, 'apart from the absence of the College Green assembly, changes were ostensibly minimal. The institution of the viceroy and his court continued. The balance of power between viceroy and chief secretary remained variable [and] above all, the Castle continued'.[1]

As a parish, Clonsilla was also to experience some change. While the local gentry and power structures remained on the whole intact, there was nonetheless a significant change in the nature and outlook of the parish in the periods prior to and immediately after the rebellion. In this chapter, the effect of the rebellion on the parish of Clonsilla will be measured by analyzing the changes to the local power structures which took place. The activities of key local figures during these years will also be examined, as will the continued threats to security and property which persisted in the parish in the aftermath of the rebellion. The Farmers' Society in Castleknock began to make significant progress in relation to the humanitarian ideology which underpinned the resolutions and rhetoric in evidence during their initial meetings, a mission made all but impossible due to the disturbances at the close of the 18th century. No investigation of the area in the aftermath of the rebellion would be complete without taking these factors into careful consideration.

Luke White, a Dublin bookseller who resided in Dawson Street, was one individual who benefited enormously due to the change which occurred in Clonsilla after the rebellion. Local folklore recorded that he had the good fortune to acquire a winning lottery ticket, which he was reputed to have found by chance. It is more likely that he lent a large sum of money to the government at a highly favourable return. Whether his fortune was amassed through enterprise, lending or opportunism, he managed to realize it at a time when the much maligned earl of Carhampton was seeking to sell his family's 450-year-old castle and estate at Luttrellstown.[2] Carhampton removed himself to his English estates at Painshill in Surrey. Despite living there until his death in 1821, the *Dublin Evening Post* reported his passing on 5 May 1811. When he instructed the newspaper to correct their error, they did so four days later under the headline 'Public Disappointment'. The passing of a decade had not helped to redeem Carhampton's reputation in Ireland, as the editor's printed apology bears witness. It read:

> It had been announced (and the report instantly diffused universal satisfaction in Ireland) that Henry Lawless Luttrell, earl of Carhampton, had departed this mortal life on the fifth of last month. The feeling arose not from revengeful motives, but from an opinion that providence had kindly interfered.
>
> The noble earl is still alive. His Lordship has therefore yet an opportunity of displaying, in the decrepitude of old age, such novelties as may rival the most celebrated actions of his youth or manhood.[3]

Having amassed a fortune far beyond any he could have aspired to during his working life, Luke White used his new found wealth to purchase the discounted property. Conscious of the depth of hatred against the Luttrells in the area, he changed the name of the estate to Woodlands, which it remained for almost 100 years until the original name was reinstated by one of his descendants. It can only be presumed that White did not continue his former career as a bookseller. It is probable that, unlike his predecessor, he spent most of his time resident on his newly-acquired estate and was always likely to seek to play a more active role within the parish.

It is difficult to assess just how the gentry of Clonsilla viewed the new arrival in their midst. They appear to have been almost unique as a group in that they genuinely held Lord Carhampton in considerable esteem. The headstone of Henry Lawes McFarland stands next to that of his father, Francis, in Clonsilla graveyard. Henry Lawes Luttrell was, of course, the baptismal name of the earl. It is worth remembering, at this point, that many of the local gentry in Clonsilla appear not to have been born in the parish. Francis McFarland, according to his headstone, was formerly of Cowley Place in Dublin and Alexander Kirkpatrick had bought Robert Bolton's estate at Coolmine in 1782. His family were said to be wealthy wool merchants who had originated in Scotland.[4] Robert Wynne had been born on his family's Hazelwood estate in Co. Sligo. Walter Troy was certainly born in the locality, but he appears to have been viewed with a certain level of either contempt or apathy by his fellow gentry. Evidently, Troy's previous objections to arming the yeomanry corps had endowed him with some form of public redemption and vindication after 1798. It is noticeable that he was afforded considerably more respect by his peers in the realms of both parish politics and society business in the aftermath of the insurrection.

Wynne and Kirkpatrick were re-appointed as church wardens of Clonsilla for another year on 14 May 1799. During the ploughing match organized by the Farmers' Society in July of that year, James Brassington judged John Archibald, a ploughman of McFarlands, to be 'the best ploughman with horses', for which Archibald received two guineas.[5] At a vestry meeting in Clonsilla on 5 September, it was decided that the roof of the church was in such bad repair that it was necessary to replace it entirely with a new slated structure. Empowered to carry out this task were the church wardens and Luke White. A subscription was necessary in order to raise funds for the project and, as had been the case previously, the amount contributed by each individual was dependant on their own personal wealth. Of the three men charged with carrying out the task, White contributed £22 11s. 0d., Kirkpatrick donated half that amount and Wynne's contribution was half that of Kirkpatrick's. It is interesting to note that Francis McFarland Jnr had begun to appear on registries and subscription lists independently of his father around this time.[6] He had testified against George Cummins at his court martial in the previous year. In October 1799, a letter from the Society for Promoting the Comforts of the Poor was sent to the Farmers' Society, requesting 'to enquire into the state of the labouring classes in the union of Castleknock'. A six-man committee consisting of the Revd David O'Connor, Luke White, Alexander Kirkpatrick, Francis McFarland, David Bricketh and Robert Wynne was appointed for that purpose.[7]

As the 19th century dawned, it was decided during a 27 January 1800 meeting of the Farmers' Society to 'hand over to the Revd Doctor O'Connor the sum of £10, in order to make an experiment of a village shop'. O'Connor, vicar of Clonsilla church, had to 'refund the same on or before 30 April next and … [was] requested to report the result of said experiment on the above day'. Two competing village shops were opened in Castleknock on 26 February 1800 by Christopher Bentley and Andrew Comber. Two months later, O'Connor reported that Bentley had sold goods amounting to the value of £10 4s. 7d. and Comber had outsold him by over £18. O'Connor believed at this early stage of the experiment that he was 'induced to think that if these shops were carried on upon a more extensive scale, they would be productive of considerable advantage to the poor'.[8]

Luke White's desire to be active in the public life of Clonsilla and the wider community is evidenced by the way he attempted to breathe new life into the Association for the Protection of Private Property during a meeting at the Royal Exchange on 10 March 1800. The Association had met infrequently and entered into no meaningful business in quite some time but White's appearance had inspired a new set of resolutions to be approved. The same fervour with which the Association had been established was again in evidence as the scribe hastily noted the minutes of the 'extraordinary meeting'. Social disorder had reached such a scale within the area that it was felt necessary to employ a constable, 'vested with the proper authority', who was to be paid a sufficient salary to allow him, in turn, employ assistants in order to help police the locality. It was further resolved that 'any person who shall refuse his [the constable's] aid and assistance, on any sudden emergency, shall be considered as an enemy to the peace and tranquillity of this neighbourhood'. While the consequences of being considered 'an enemy' can be presumed to have been severe, obedience and cooperation was also actively encouraged. Any servant or labourer who would 'faithfully aid and assist his master or employer in the defence of his house if attacked by Banditti, or the successful pursuit and recovery of his master's property'[9] was to be suitably rewarded by the Association.

On 28 April 1800, Thomas Kernan, described as 'Robert Wynne's man', was given a one guinea premium by the Farmers' Society for 'having been the most expert in his different kinds of work'.[10] Kernan had previously been appointed as a parish constable by the Association for the Protection of Private Property in 1794. On 24 July of that year, a child of the same name, most likely Kernan's son, was recorded as having been buried in the parish.[11] It was common practice at that time for a father to pass on his name to his son. Indeed, McFarland, Wynne and Kirkpatrick all had male children who bore their own Christian names. Wynne's sympathy for Kernan was unsurprising as his own son, James, was born in 1800 and died the same year. The Wynne's had lost another son, Sydenham, a few years previously. There were a high number of children buried in the parish around this time, and the vestry minute book of that year described the period from 27 December 1799 to 31 August 1800 as 'a year of great calamity and distress'. A subscription totalling £299 13s. 16d. was amassed from the gentry of the parish, in order to supply the poor of the area with fuel and provision at a reduced price.[12] An example of six such items is displayed in Table 2.

Table 2. Examples of provision and fuel sold to the poor at reduced price

	Prime Cost	Sold For
Oaten Meal	£939 7s. 7d.	£705 9s. 8d.
Rye	£11 0s. 0d.	£10 2s. 6d.
Turf	£87 3s. 9d.	£32 5s. 10d.
Bacon	£12 0s. 8d.	£12 0s. 8d.
Candles	£5 8s. 2d.	£4 5s. 6d.
Tobacco	£5 3s. 0d.	£5 9s. 0d.

On the same day that Kernan received one guinea from the Society, several premiums were also distributed to other deserving members of the community.

Two examples of which were the £3 8s. 3d. that was to be divided equally between Anne Darcy and Susan Walsh for 'having done the greatest number of days work in husbandry during the year'. An equivalent amount was given to numerous local children, for having been 'the best conducted children in their respective schools'. Among those pupils to receive this sizable premium were John Riley in Castleknock, Peter Lynch, John Martin and Mary Divine in Blanchardstown and John Kearney, Martin Brady and Mary Brady in Porterstown. To put that amount in context, the annual salary of the clerk of Clonsilla church was still £10 in 1800. The following month, Wynne was appointed to head a committee instructed to carry out a study into the agricultural improvements that had taken place in the locality during the previous year.[13]

It was decided by the members of the Society to meet at 11 o'clock in Alexander Kirkpatrick's house at Coolmine on Tuesday, 8 July, after the ploughing match organized for that day. This competition appears to have become an important date in the social calendar of the community in a relatively short space of time. The premiums offered to the labouring classes in these events would surely have excited their interests and there seems to have been a considerable amount of pride taken by the local gentry when one of their 'men' was successful in their chosen field. The likelihood is that the competing labouring classes trained and prepared for the ploughing matches in the time leading up to the competition. In order to win the first premium offered it was necessary merely to be adjudged 'the best ploughman' with either horse or oxen. By 1800, a clear set of rules and stipulations had emerged in order to achieve that title. By analyzing the notes and additions contained in the Society journal entries over a three year period, the rules for the ploughing match of 8 July 1800 can be stated to have been as follows:

- An independent judge must be appointed to preside over the ploughing match
- An equal portion of ground must be measured for each candidate
- Each ploughman must plough three ridges
- One ridge must be left unploughed between each division
- Whoever performs this task in the most efficient manner shall obtain the premium
- If necessary, whoever is adjudged to have performed this task in the best manner shall obtain the premium

The evolution of the rules which governed these events is indicative of the fact that the standard of performance had risen since the first competition and tighter regulation was required to assess the candidates. There may also have been some contentious decisions and disputed outcomes at previous events. Four men entered the competition for 'best ploughman with horses' on the day in question. They were Christopher Kelly, who worked for Walter Troy, an employee of Henry Blackwood by the name of Brain Floody, and James and John Dwyer, both of whom were workers on Francis McFarland's farm. McFarland and the Dwyers ultimately lost out on that day, as Kelly and Floody, 'being equal in merit', shared the two guinea premium on offer. The equivalent competition using oxen was a somewhat farcical event as Laurence Hall, being the only competitor, was given the premium for 'the degree of skill displayed in performing his task'.[14] Evidently the use of oxen for ploughing was not as simple a task as Lieutenant Archer had described in his statistical survey.

Luke White presided over another 'extraordinary meeting' of the Association for the Protection of Private Property, this time held in Clonsilla on 10 August 1800.[15] Association business had been slow since the dramatic 10 March meeting during which White had announced his arrival with a series of resolutions and promises. Unfortunately for White, who seemed to have possessed unparalleled good fortune, his wife did not have long to enjoy their new life and died on 8 July at just 40 years of age.[16] He had now to raise the couple's six children, Henry, George, Elizabeth, Emelia, John and Matilda, without the assistance of his deceased spouse. The children ranged in age from two to 14 and White was to survive his wife by 24 years.[17] The gratefulness of those present was expressed to Mr Harrison, for his 'trouble and attention in carrying out the protection of Nicholas Byrne for stealing a cow belonging to John Connell'. The following Sunday, Thomas Blair resigned as secretary and Richard Carpenter-Smith was appointed in his place. At some point in the week after that meeting, one of the lodges belonging to Luke White was attacked by a number of armed men and a steward of White's, a man by the name of Byrne, was robbed of a gun and gun powder. This was a prime example of the activities of the 'banditti', former rebels who had evaded capture and refused to lay down their arms or submit to an oath to the crown. They existed, to a large extent, on the fringes of society and the threat that they posed to local security was substantial. The Sunday meeting subsequent to the attack offered £50 for a prosecution in this case and 20 guineas for disclosing private information. The final entry into the Association minute book, one week later, simply stated 'Association met but did not enter into business'.[18] August 1800 saw four successive meetings of the Association being held on Sundays in Clonsilla. This pattern ended and the Association ceased when the property of Luke White could not be protected. Robert Weir and James Halpin, both previously unconnected with the parish, were admitted to the Association along with White at the 10 March meeting. Thomas Blair's replacement as secretary may also have been introduced to the Association by White as he had never previously held any position of responsibility in the community. The local gentry who had taken such prominent civic roles in the years which preceded the rebellion are unlikely to have reacted favourably to this situation and it is conceivable that the Association crumbled as internal parish squabbling made it impossible for it to function.

Luke White's descendants were to play an important role in the parish during the 19th century. Elected as MP for Co. Leitrim, his fourth son was granted a peerage and bestowed with the title of Lord Annaly. The family played host to Queen Victoria on two occasions, when she visited and took tea by the demesne's waterfall in 1844 and 1900. White's great grandson, the 3rd Lord Annaly, restored the name of Luttrellstown to the estate. Although the ownership of the estate has changed hands on many occasions since then, the name of the grounds has remained the same.

The report requested by the Farmers' Society into the progress after seven months of the competing village shops was delivered by David O'Connor on 31 October 1800. Initially, Andrew Comber appeared to be outselling his counterpart, Christopher Bentley, by a considerable amount. At this stage, however, Bentley had sold articles to the amount of £262 5s. 2d. whereas Comber's intake amounted to £77 0s. 11d. Bentley's shop had, in that time, made a tidy profit of £22 11s. 3d. for the Society and no explanation was given or alluded to as to why this reversal in fortunes had taken place. The complete list of articles sold in the shops at this time, those being the ones most desired and required by the labouring classes, was as follows:

herrings	soaps and candles	tobacco and snuff
starch	bread and butter	tea and sugar
thread and pins	pepper and salt	liquorice and pipes

Upon hearing the report, the members of the Society duly decided to recall the £5 loan advanced to Comber and forward it to Bentley, whose own £5 loan was extended by a further six months. Bentley was to continue in the position 'on act of his punctuality, diligence and honesty', while Comber's shop was shut down. The following month, Bentley was also appointed as clerk of Clonsilla church after the death of William Dobbs.[19] It is unsurprising to find that in the mindset of post rebellion Irish society, the consequences of failure were to be severe in the extreme.

The scheme for the planned refurbishment and slating of Clonsilla church had hit serious financial difficulties, as evidenced by a vestry meeting held on 21 November 1800. The cost incurred at that stage amounted to £185 11s. 2d., meaning that the project had already run almost £100 over budget.[20] A second subscription was deemed necessary and an identical one to that raised on 5 September 1799 was again requested from the parishioners. Wynne had proved himself to be a very effective administrator when he ascended to the role of church warden in place of Walter Troy in 1794 and had managed the church accounts particularly well during that time. As a Roman Catholic and brother to the archbishop of Dublin, Troy's position as warden of the local established church may well have been resented and questioned regardless of his dubious handling of the vestry accounts. As such, Wynne showed a particular ruthlessness and cunning in removing him from that position. Walter Troy's own grave in Blanchardstown is often confused with that of his eldest brother's, owing to the acknowledgment to him on the headstone.[21] The archbishop once described his younger sibling as 'an unabashed, busy, intermeddling person'[22] and it seems that even in death and memoriam, his considerable power cast a dark and lingering shadow over his brother.

Wynne's effective handling of the process of enlarging the church had encouraged the vestry to allow him complete autonomy in spending church money in enclosing the church grounds with a wall. When he did so successfully, parish revenues were considerably raised due to an acceptable increase in burial fees. Wynne had displayed an ability to work with Kirkpatrick since he assumed the role of church warden in 1796. The two indicated that they also held a preference to work together when they established and commanded the ill-fated Clonsilla yeomanry corps in that year. The two established wardens were joined on their latest enterprise by Luke White, by order of vestry, perhaps reflecting the financial problems the project was encountering. Various factors may also have resulted in the disintegration of the Association for the Protection of Private Property, but all evidence seems to suggest that Clonsilla, at this time, was becoming a parish rife in internal squabbles and fall-outs, to the detriment of all those involved.

In order to make the maintenance work economically viable, it was decided that those seats and pews in the church not yet assigned were to be 'sold forthwith'. Owing to this decision, it was necessary to compile a list of available seats and pews within the church and also to indicate which seats were already assigned to members of the congregation. The position of a family's pew, so often an indication of their standing within the community, was listed in order by the name of its senior male member. Francis McFarland held the first pew, and Kirkpatrick, White and Wynne held the second, third and forth respectively. The latter three each held a second pew at the back of the church, whereas McFarland's seems to have been assigned to his son of the same name. It is also interesting to note that the only seats assigned to the clergy were in the fourteenth row of the church.[23] The elder McFarland's grave is located at the back of Clonsilla church, beside that of Luke White, the inscription on which reads:

> As a mark of filial love and of respect for the memory of dear and honoured parents, this stone is erected to Francis McFarland and his beloved wife Mary, both of Cowley place, Dublin.
> The former of whom departed this life on 23 March 1817, aged 90. The latter on 28 March 1817, surviving him only 36 hours.

Wynne and Kirkpatrick were issued with medals by the Farmers' Society on 26 January 1801 for 'preserving their offices and farmyards in the neatest and most exact order'. The former was also to receive a medal for having the best constructed barn in the first class. During the course of that day's meeting, the committee of Wynne, Kirkpatrick, McFarland and Troy, appointed to investigate the improvements in agricultural practice amongst members, report their findings to the Society. The comprehensive detail which this account provides includes vital information on the state of the most important sector of the local economy in the post rebellion era. The committee members were quick to compliment themselves on the constructions of their corn stands, which they believed were all secured from vermin in the best possible manner. However, it was noted that 'if anyone claimed to have a preferred, it was that of Robert Wynne's, from the solidity of its construction and judicious disposal of a number of parallel walls, open at both sides'. The superior condition of Wynne's barn also attracted the praise of the Society's members.

McFarland, it was recognized, had erected the only threshing machine in the neighbourhood, 'with a corn fan beneath, worked by the same machine'. The machine was an object of much attention to the Society as it is reported to have answered 'the most sanguine of expectation.' Wynne received further acknowledgment for having imported two Leicestershire breed cows at considerable expense to himself, while Luke White, the committee noted, 'has collected several thousand loads of compost'. The report having been concluded, Kirkpatrick requested that he be struck off several committees of which he was a member.[24]

After 1798, Wynne seems to have devoted most of his time to employing innovative agricultural methods on his farm and receiving considerable recognition for his efforts. Lieutenant Joseph Archer, in his statistical survey of Co. Dublin in 1801, stated:

> Robert Wynne at Clonsilla is extensive also in potato husbandry; at my last visit, 16 acres, mostly in drills, were almost finished. Some of his neighbours vie with him in their exertions, and many other parts of the country have made the most laudable efforts of imitation … If a favourable harvest should succeed these endeavours, we may next year hail the happy return of plenty.

Details of a competition to produce the best bull and heifer in the Co. Dublin by 8 April 1802 were recorded. Six farmers in the county as whole had entered, two of whom were Wynne and White. Unfortunately, the result of this competition is not known. Archer also revealed that Wynne was a member of the Dublin Farmers' Society, which would explain his reduced participation in the local society and non-involvement in the village shop initiative. It can only be presumed that Wynne was engaged in a similar strategy of networking and political endeavour, but at a wider community level to that which had seen him achieve such respect and favourable reputation amongst his peers in the parish. The standing committee of that Society included his older brothers, Owen Wynne and the Revd Richard Wynne, as well as Samuel Garnett, the Clonee farmer whose 125 sheep had provided food for the rebels encamped on the Hill of Tara in May 1798.[25] A list of fairs contained in the survey revealed that there were two 'horse and pedlary' fairs held every year in Luttrellstown, on 28 March and 4 September. The survey also contains an interesting account of the dangers faced by farmers who came into the markets in Dublin city, such as Smithfield, to sell their produce. Archer described the 'most destructive practice' of 'forestalling' which prevails in the city, by which, 'there is a class of men that make a livelihood of this business'. They are, he believed, 'so ingenious in the practice of it, that they frequently pass the cows through two or three hands, even in the same market, before the dairymen can get hold of them'.[26]

Wynne and Kirkpatrick were re-appointed as church wardens at a meeting of the vestry on 7 April 1801 and Christopher Bentley remained as clerk. Despite the collection of a second subscription, the funds of the parish were deemed inadequate to complete the necessary repairs to the church, which were said to have been left unfinished. The following year, Wynne and Kirkpatrick jointly resigned from their positions and Luke White and Thomas Kinsley took their place as wardens. Wynne, who did not attend the meeting, appears to have left the parish around this time.[27] On 24 May, the Farmers' Society unanimously declared him an honorary member and his name ceased to appear on any of the local registers. On 7 June, at a vestry meeting, his pew and seats in Clonsilla church were assigned to fellow Dublin Farmers' Society member Samuel Garnett,[28] whose wife Mary had been buried in May of that year.[29] During that meeting, the Revd David O'Connor complained 'whereas it appears that the late church wardens, not having made the repairs ordered by act of vestry, it is resolved that present wardens be empowered to complete said repairs'. In addition to these repairs, it was decided to erect a new gate, to put new shutters on the vestry and belfry windows, to apply two new coats of paint and purchase a new lock with two keys. While not expressly stated, it can only be presumed that White was to fund these improvements in the financially-strained parish.

Whereas Wynne had used Walter Troy's dubious handling of the church funds as a means of furthering his position within the community, it seems now that the difficulties which were apparent in the repair project were similarly used by White to assert his capabilities as parish administrator. Unfortunately for O'Connor, the stability which Wynne and Kirkpatrick had brought to the parish was not to be recovered until George Vesey, who owned much of the land between Clonsilla and Lucan, assumed the role of warden in 1808. White did not attend any vestry meetings and was replaced in 1803 by Andrew Roche and William Smith. By Easter of the following year, O'Connor had written to the Protestant archbishop of Dublin to complain that Clonsilla required the appointment of new wardens. The archbishop's response was to recommend Smith and Thomas Bryan for the position. On 15 April 1805, Bryan and John Clarke undertook the responsibilities only for Smith to return the following year, where he remained for some time. His co-warden changed on a yearly basis until the appointment of Vesey in 1808, which marked the return of some stability and consistency to parish affairs.[30]

In Wynne, the parish of Clonsilla was fortunate to have found a capable and ambitious administrator who appeared to have carried out his duties with the utmost attention and diligence. While it is fair to say that he displayed a remarkable awareness of how to manipulate situations to suit his own interests, it is clear that whichever body or Association he used for this purpose benefited enormously from his considerable talents. The relative turmoil of the vestry meetings prior to and immediately after his career as warden is testament to this fact. Alexander Kirkpatrick never resumed the level of involvement in local affairs that he had engaged in during the years that Wynne was active in the parish, despite remaining there until his death in August 1818.[31] Where his ambition had clouded his judgment, Wynne's reputation was publicly and severely compromised. It is as unfair, however, to view the defection of many members of his yeomanry corps as a reflection on his abilities as a military commander as it is to equate his role in promoting progressive methods of potato farming to responsibility for the famine of the 1840s. Disaffection and sedition among the ranks of the yeomanry were commonplace throughout the country and many had joined with the expressed intention of being trained and armed in order to rise against the government when the time should arrive. Few commanders would have had to counter quite the depth of hatred that a local landlord such as Carhampton could evoke among the labouring classes. Wynne's own conduct, in rescuing Hamilton George in Ratoath, was exemplary in its efficiency and bravery and he must have felt an initial sense of pride and vindication in his corps, until the full extent of what had been occurring under his command became apparent in the next few days.

After the rebellion, Wynne appears to have immersed himself in his primary function in life as a farmer. Despite his prominent family background, the monetary amounts he entered into the various subscriptions required of the Associations and Societies show him to have been a prosperous farmer of moderate personal wealth. Archer's listing of the most prominent 100 or so estates in Dublin did not include Wynne's,[32] yet his ability to compete in a shared realm of enterprise and ambition made him one of the most important farmers in the county. Wynne's departure from the community left a void that proved difficult to fill and the extent of his contribution to the parish must surely have been evident to the Revd O'Connor when he wrote to the archbishop at Easter 1804. Wynne, who was said to have been one time Steward of the Vice-Regal Household at Dublin Castle, was appointed a Commissioner of Port Duties and Customs in Ireland on 15 July 1807, with an annual salary of £1,000. His administrative abilities obviously did not go unnoticed to those in a position to reward generously. In addition to this handsome income, he was also legally entitled to pay 'any other person or persons such sums of monies for salaries or rewards', effectively allowing him to dispose of his income by delegating his duties to others and paying them as he saw fit.[33]

In total, Elizabeth Wynne gave birth to 15 children between the years of 1791 and 1810. However, the couple were to suffer considerable personal tragedy in the years ahead. In 1812, their ten-year-old son Charles became the third Wynne child to die. The 1820s proved a further difficult time for the family as both Mark and Louisa died in 1824, aged 16 and 11 respectively. Their son Robert lived to become a Church of Ireland minister, before passing away at the age of 35 in 1826. The death of 17-year-old Owen in 1827 was followed two years later by that of 15-year-old Caroline. Robert Wynne resided in Kingstown (as Dun Laoghaire was renamed in 1821) at the time of his wife Elizabeth's passing on 26 May 1834. He himself died there on 31 May 1838.[34] Tragedy and suffering, barely comparable to that experienced in modern Ireland, was a reality of life for families from every section of society. Twentieth-century retellings of Irish history promote the idea that such hardships were the exclusive preserve of the poor and the destitute. As the case of the Wynnes should illustrate, financial security could not prevent a family from experiencing the most severe instances of loss and desolation.

George Cummins, the state prisoner, was released from his detention in Fort George along with the other state prisoners on 30 June 1802.[35] Nothing is known of his namesake and former Clonsilla yeoman, although a 'Mr Cummins' does appear on the parish register for Castleknock in 1801, but includes no other detail.[36] In accordance with letters conveyed out of the lord lieutenant's office after his court martial, it is probable that he found himself in the ranks of the British army for his penance. After the other Cummins' release from custody, he was reported to have made his way to Hamburg with several of the ex-state prisoners, including Samuel Neilson and Matthew Dowling, where they were reported to have been in August 1802.[37] He arrived in New York in late 1802, where, in the opinion of fellow Ulsterman John Caldwell, being 'an eminent surgical character, strongly recommended, with good certs from Edinburgh ... [he] could could not fail of succeeding'.[38] Despite this, he was evidently dissatisfied with his New York practice as only an outbreak of yellow fever in the city prevented him from accepting a 'competency' from a wealthy friend in Natchez, Mississippi. When Thomas

Emmet also settled in the city, he decided to remain.[39] On 1 October 1807, he was a signatory to an address presented by the Hibernian Providential Society of New York to Matilda Tone, widow of Theobald Wolfe Tone, which read:

> To many of us he [Tone] was intimately known; by all of us he was ardently beloved. Wherever Irishmen dare to express the sentiments of their hearts, they celebrate the name and sufferings of Tone. We are likewise directed to present a sword to his youthfull son and successor, with a lively hope, that it may one day, in his hand, avenge the wrongs of his country.[40]

Cummins was later to become involved in harnessing and directing the Irish vote in New York, with other former United Irishmen, towards the Clintonian faction of Republican politics.[41] He lived in the city during the period immortalized by Herbert Ausbury in his book, *The Gangs of New York,* although it is unlikely that he had much involvement with the 'Dead Rabbit' or 'Plug Ugly' gangs of that era.

Christopher Bentley's village shop in Castleknock reported a profit of £31 9s. 0d. in 1802. A total of £211 worth of bread was sold in the preceding year, as well as 2,602 lbs of butter, 252 lbs of tea, 139 stones of sugar and 172 lbs of tobacco. In 1803, the total intake of the shop was £882 10s. 1d., amounting to a profit of £60 03s. 2d.[42] The establishment of the village shops by the Society reveals many crucial details about the mindset of the local gentry living in that era. The shop must surely have been of great convenience to the local labouring classes and at times of hardship it was used to distribute the essentials to those most in need at a reduced price. In 1801, when the annual ploughing match had to be postponed due to 'the great drought of weather and consequent hardening of the ground', Bentley's shop reported no profit due to 'premiums for the poor and reductions'. By addressing issues of poverty, the members were also securing their privileged positions against the likelihood of further upheaval and attack by an oppressed majority. Their seemingly kind actions strengthened their control over the lives and fortunes of their tenants and workers, whom they believed would be contented if their basic needs were provided for. Enterprise and ambition, it appears, were to be constantly and actively encouraged. The rewards and premiums offered for expertise in the vast array of labouring activities indicated a desire to foster, amongst the labouring class, an incentive and pride in their work which stretched beyond a need to graft to survive. These premiums and rewards were also obtained by achievements that were in keeping with the ideology, values and beliefs of the Society's members. On 26 April 1804, Bentley reported to the Society that 'by their kindness and blessing of providence, he [Bentley] has acquired such a capital as will hereafter enable him to carry out his business without trespassing farther on their liberality.'

In 1805, he reported a profit of £135 10s. 11d. to the Society, who in turn offered to pay his licence for the previous year and 'hereafter, so long as his merit shall appear to deserve it'. The final entry in the Society meeting book, which appears to have been made by Bentley himself in a particularly neat and decorative hand, was an account of the items sold in the shop in 1805. In addition to the products first available in 1800, bacon, wheatmeal, oatmeal, potatoes, soup, linen, corduroy, mustard, pepper, eggs, milk and sugar candy were now obtainable by the labourers of the area.[43]

The treatment of Bentley is perhaps the clearest illustration of the mentality of the gentry in the post rebellion barony of Castleknock. While enterprise and ambition was to be encouraged, to fail was to be damned. Andrew Comber, the failed entrepreneur, whose situation by modern values would be deemed most suitable for compassion and kindness, had his £5 loan recalled at his most desperate hour, only to see it lent out to the victor. Bentley then went on to receive gainful employment as a church clerk and constant support from the Society in maintaining his favourable position. Given that the members were the survivors and veterans of an attempt to obliterate their class' existence and wealth, it is unsurprising that their outlook was prone to such extremities of opinion and action.

Leabharlanna Poibli Chathair Bhaile Átha Cliath
Leabharlanna Poibli Chathair Bhaile Átha Cliath
Dublin City Public Libraries

Notes

ABBREVIATIONS

BL   British Library
DEP   *Dublin Evening Post*
FJ   *Freeman's Journal*
NAI   National Archives of Ireland
NLI   National Library of Ireland
TNA   The National Archives, London
RCB   Representative Church Body Library
TCD   Trinity College Dublin

INTRODUCTION

1   James Kelly, 'Conservative Protestant political thought in late eighteenth-century Ireland' in S. J. Connolly (ed.), *Political ideas in eighteenth-century Ireland* (Dublin, 2000), p. 185.
2   R.F. Foster, *Modern Ireland, 1600–1971* (London, 1989), p. 265.
3   R.B. McDowell, 'The protestant nation' in T.W. Moody and F.X. Martin (eds), *The course of Irish history* (Cork, 1967), p. 233.
4   Samuel Lewis, *A topographical dictionary of Ireland* (London, 1837), p. 375.
5   Margaret E. Crawford, *Counting the people* (Dublin, 2003), p. 51.
6   Irish census data available at: Enhanced Parliamentary Papers on Ireland 1801–1922, http://www.bopcris.ac.uk/eppi_censusdata.html [10 December 2006].

1. CIVIC INITIATIVE AND PARISH POLITICS IN CLONSILLA, 1792–7

1   Weston St John Joyce, *Lucan and its neighbourhood* (Dublin, 1901), p. 6.
2   NLI, Longfield maps 21/F/51/66.

3   Charles and Mary Hulgraine, *St Mochta's church, Porterstown* (Dublin, 1990), p. 35.
4   Francis Elrington Ball, *A history of the county Dublin ... part fourth* (Dublin, 1902), p. 3.
5   James O'Driscoll, *Cnucha: a history of Castleknock and district* (Dublin, 1977), p. 116.
6   Jim Lacey, *Candle in the window* (Dublin, 1999), p. 40.
7   O'Driscoll, *Cnucha,* p. 40.
8   Higgins to Cooke, 29 December 1796: NAI, Rebellion papers, 620/18/14.
9   Thomas Bartlett (ed.), *Revolutionary Dublin, 1795–1801,* (Dublin, 2004), p. 24.
10 RCB, Minute book of the Association of the Inhabitants of the United Parishes of Castleknock, Leixlip, Chapelizod and Dunboyne. P.0352.28/2.
11 RCB, Vestry minute book for Clonsilla, 1705–1800. P.0353.05/1.
12 RCB, P.0352.28/2.
13 Jim Lacey, *Candle in the window* (Dublin, 1999), p. 66.
14 NLI, Gen. Off. MS 495
15 RCB, P.0352.28/2.
16 NLI, Longfield maps 21/F/51/64
17 RCB, P.0352.28/2.
18 Ibid.
19 Ibid.

20   *FJ*, 6 Sept. 1792.
21   RCB, P.0353.05/1.
22   RCB, P.0352.28/2.
23   Winston Guthrie Jones, *The Wynnes of Sligo and Leitrim* (Leitrim, 1994), p. 5.
24   NLI, Gen. Off. MS 495.
25   In conversation with David Parsons, genealogist and 2nd great grandson of Robert Wynne.
26   RCB, P.0353.05/1.
27   Charles and Mary Hulgraine, *St Mochta's church, Porterstown* (Dublin, 1990), p. 30.
28   RCB, P.0353.05/1.
29   Ibid.
30   Ibid.
31   RCB, P.0353.05/1.
32   RCB, P.0352.28/2.
33   Thomas Bartlett (ed.), *Revolutionary Dublin, 1795–1801* (Dublin, 2004), p. 102.
34   Bartlett (ed.), *Revolutionary Dublin*, p. 23.
35   *FJ*, 20 Sept. 1792.
36   Ibid.
37   Kevin Whelan, 'The United Irishmen, the Enlightenment and popular culture' in Dickson, Keogh and Whelan (eds), *The United Irishmen: republicanism, radicalism and rebellion* (Dublin, 1996).
38   James Kelly, *Proceedings of the Irish House of Lords 1771–1800* (Dublin, 2008), p. 11.
39   Ibid.
40   Ibid.
41   RCB, P.0353.05/1
42   Ibid.
43   *FJ*, 6 Oct. 1796.
44   As told by Nick McAuley and Michael Kelly to Michael Kenny in Michael Kenny, 'Dunboyne in 1798' in Dunboyne Historical Society, *Dunboyne, Kilbride and Clonee – A picture of the past* (Dublin, 1989), p. 10.
45   R.B. McDowell, *Ireland in the age of imperialism and revolution, 1760–1801* (Oxford, 1979), p. 557.
46   R.B. McDowell, 'The Protestant nation' in T.W. Moody and F.X. Martin (eds), *The course of Irish history* (Cork, 1967), p. 232.
47   *FJ*, 7 Oct. 1796.
48   *FJ*, 20 Oct. 1796.
49   *FJ*, 22 Oct. 1796.

50   NAI, Rebellion Papers 620/18/14 .
51   RCB, P.0353.05/1.
52   Richard Musgrave, *Memoirs of the different rebellions in Ireland* … (2nd ed., Dublin, 1801),p. 175.
53   Ibid., p. 176.
54   Centre for Kentish Studies, Camden Papers U840015 6A/7.
55   BL, Add. MSS 33103 fos. 130–1.
56   RCB, P.35228.3.
57   RCB, P.0352.28/2.
58   NAI, IWR/1833/F/617.
59   Musgrave, *Memoirs of the different rebellions in Ireland* …, p. 277.
60   Lt Joseph Archer, *Archer's statistical survey of the county of Dublin* (Dublin, 1801), p. 205.
61   RCB, P.35228.3.

2. LOCAL EXPERIENCE OF THE 1798
REBELLION

1   Ibid.
2   Ibid.
3   RCB, P.35228.3.
4   Lt Joseph Archer, *Archer's statistical survey of the county of Dublin* (Dublin, 1801), p. 205.
5   Ibid., p. 137.
6   McDowell, *Ireland in the age of imperialism and revolution (1760–1801)*, p. 558.
7   Ruán O'Donnell, *1798 diary* (Dublin, 1998), p. 210.
8   NAI, R.P. 620/32/89.
9   Mario Corrigan, *All that delirium of the brave: Kildare in 1798* (Naas, 1998), p. 24.
10   NAI, R.P. 620/32/89.
11   Michael Durey, *Transatlantic radicals and the early American Republic* (Kansas, 1997), p. 128.
12   Stella Tillyard, *Citizen Lord: the life of Edward FitzGerald* (New York, 1997), p. 250.
13   Liam Chambers, 'The 1798 rebellion in North Leinster' in Thomas Bartlett, David Dickson, Dáire Keogh and Kevin Whelan (eds), *1798 – A bicentenary perspective* (Dublin, 2003), p. 122.
14   RCB, P.35228.3.
15   *FJ*, 12 May 1797.

16 NAI, R.P. Higgins to Cooke, 18 May 1798 620/18/14.

17 Bartlett (ed.), *Revolutionary Dublin*, p. 30.

18 NAI, R.P. 620/18/14.

19 Richard Musgrave, *Memoirs of the different rebellions in Ireland* ... (2nd ed., Dublin, 1801), p. 276.

20 Steen, *The battle of the Hill of Tara*, p. 12.

21 Musgrave, *Memoirs of the different rebellions in Ireland* ..., p. 276.

22 Michael Kenny, 'Dunboyne in 1798' in *Dunboyne, Kilbride and Clonee: a picture of the past*, p. 11.

23 *FJ*, 25 May 1796.

24 RCB, Vestry minute book for Dunboyne. P.05605.1.2.

25 NAI, R.P. 'The Court Martial of Thomas Connor and Thomas Atkinson in Dublin Castle, 12 July 1798' 620/3/16/14.

26 NAI R.P. 620/3/16/14.

27 NAI R.P. 620/38/56.

28 Michael Kenny, 'Dunboyne in 1798' in *Dunboyne, Kilbride and Clonee*, p. 11.

29 Chambers, 'The 1798 rebellion in North Leinster' in Bartlett et al., (eds), *1798*, p. 122.

30 Ibid.

31 NAI, R.P. 620/18/14.

32 Musgrave, *Memoirs of the different rebellions in Ireland* ..., p. 277.

33 NAI, R.P. 'The court martial of George Cummins in Dublin Castle, 12 July 1798' 620/3/16/9.

34 Steen, *The battle of the Hill of Tara*.

35 *FJ*, 25 May 1798.

36 RCB, P.05605.1.2.

37 Steen, *The battle of the Hill of Tara*, p. 22.

38 Public Record Office (London), War Office 40/11. The account of Captain Blanche at the Hill of Tara.

39 The National Archives, London WO 40/11.

40 TNA, WO 40/11.

41 *FJ*, 29 May 1798.

42 Camden to Portland, 27 May 1798 (PRO, HO 100/76/258–9).

43 NAI, R.P. 620/18/14.

44 NAI, R.P. 620/3/16/9.

45 NLI, Longfield maps 21/F/51/64.

46 RCB, P.0353.05/1.

47 NAI, R.P. 620/3/16/9.

48 NAI, R.P. 620/18/14.

49 NAI, R.P. 620/18/14.

50 NLI, Kilmainham Papers, MS 1133/14.

51 NLI, Kilmainham Papers, MS 1133/98.

52 RCB, P.0352.28/2.

53 RCB, P.35228.3.

54 RCB, P.035228.3.

55 NAI, R.P. 620/32/89.

56 Charles and Mary Hulgraine, *St Mochta's church, Porterstown* (Dublin, 1990), p. 32.

57 Chambers, 'The 1798 rebellion in North Leinster' in Bartlett et al., (eds), *1798*, p. 124.

58 NAI, R.P. 'Examination of Thomas Connelly, 29 May 1798' 620/3/16/14.

59 NAI, R.P. 620/38/56.

60 NAI, R.P. 620/3/16/14.

61 James Quinn, 'The Kilmainham treaty of 1798' in Bartlett et al., (eds), *1798* (Dublin, 2003), p. 435.

62 NAI, Kilmainham prisoners list, 1798. Pris 1/10/1.

63 NAI, R.P., 620/32/89.

64 Musgrave, *Memoirs of the different rebellions in Ireland* ..., p. 277.

65 Michael Durey, *Transatlantic radicals and the early American republic* (Kansas, 1907), p. 128.

66 R.R. Madden, *The United Irishmen: Their lives and times* 2 vols (London, 1843), p. 328.

3. SOCIAL CHANGE AND ECONOMIC RECOVERY AFTER THE REBELLION

1 R.F. Foster, *Modern Ireland, 1600–1971* (London, 1989), p. 289.

2 James O'Driscoll, *Cnucha: a history of Castleknock and district* (Dublin, 1977), p. 44.

3 *DEP*, 9 May 1811.

4 Jim Lacey, *Candle in the window* (Dublin, 1999), p. 66.

5 RCB, P.35228.3.

6 RCB, P.0353.05.

7 RCB, P.35228.3.

8 Ibid.

9 RCB, P.0352.28.

10 RCB, P.35228.3.

11 RCB, baptisms, marriages and burials in Castleknock, P.3521.3

12 RCB, vestry minute book for
    Clonsilla, 1800–1870. P.0353.05/2
13 RCB, P.35228.3.
14 RCB, P.0353.05.
15 RCB, P.0352.28/2.
16 RCB, P.3521.3.
17 NLI, Gen. Off. MS 495.
18 RCB, P.0352.28/2.
19 RCB, P.35228.3.
20 RCB, P.0353.05/2.
21 Hulgraine, *St Mochta's church
    Porterstown*, p. 31.
22 Bartlett (ed.), *Revolutionary Dublin*, p. 274.
23 NAI, R.P. 620/18/14.
24 RCB, P.35228.3.
25 *FJ*, 25 May 1798.
26 Archer, *Archer's statistical survey of the
    county of Dublin.*
27 RCB, P.0353.05/2.
28 RCB, P.35228.3.
29 NLI, Gen. Off. MS495.
30 RCB, P.35228.3.
31 NAI The will of Alexander
    Kirkpatrick Char 1/2/p206 (1818).

32 Archer, *Archer's statistical survey of the
    county of Dublin*, p. 93.
33 NAI, chan/old series C414, *Legal
    document appointing Robert Wynne
    Commissioner of port duties and customs
    in Ireland.*
34 NAI, IWR/1838/F/383, *the will of
    Robert Wynne.*
35 Madden, *The United Irishmen: their lives
    and times*, p. 328.
36 NLI, Gen. Off. MS 495.
37 Trinity College Dublin MS 873/560,
    Emmet's letters from Brussels,
    1802.
38 Durey, *Transatlantic radicals and the early
    American republic*, p. 184
39 Public Record Office Northern
    Ireland D/1759/3b/6/32.
40 Madden, *The United Irishmen: their lives
    and times*, p. 415.
41 Durey, *Transatlantic radicals and the early
    American republic*, p. 270.
42 RCB, P.35228.3.
43 Ibid.